David Trickey is a consultant clinical psychologist who has specialised in working with traumatised children, young people and their families since 2000. He is co-director of the UK Trauma Council, which harnesses the expertises of the UK's leading child trauma experts to produce resources for those working directly with traumatised children, young people and their families, as well as providing guidance and policy briefings based on the best available evidence. As a clinician, he continues to focus on direct clinical work and the training and supervision of other clinicians working with traumatised children and young people. He was a member of the committee responsible for the 2018 revision of the NICE Guidelines for PTSD. In all of his roles, he draws heavily on the body of research literature, to which he has made a modest contribution.

Dr Vicky Lawson is a chartered health psychologist, clinician and author who specialises in supporting behaviour change. She has a particular interest in translating research evidence into practical action.

T0054656

Helping Your Child is a series for parents and caregivers to support children through developmental difficulties, both psychological and physical. Each guide uses clinically proven techniques.

Series editors: Prof Peter Cooper and Dr Polly Waite

Titles in the series include:

Helping Your Child with Fears and Worries

Helping Your Child with Friendship Problems and Bullying

Helping Your Child with a Physical Health Condition

Helping Your Child with Sleep Problems

HELPING YOUR CHILD WITH LOSS AND TRAUMA

A Self-Help Guide for Parents

David Trickey with Vicky Lawson

ROBINSON

ROBINSON

First published in Great Britain in 2023 by Robinson

Copyright © David Trickey and Vicky Lawson, 2023

1 3 5 7 9 10 8 6 4 2

The moral rights of the authors have been asserted.

Important Note
This book is not intended as a substitute for medical advice or treatment. Any person with a condition requiring medical attention should consult a qualified medical practitioner or suitable therapist.

All rights reserved.
No part of this publication may be reproduced, stored in a retrieval system, or transmitted, in any form, or by any means, without the prior permission in writing of the publisher, nor be otherwise circulated in any form of binding or cover other than that in which it is published and without a similar condition including this condition being imposed on the subsequent purchaser.

A CIP catalogue record for this book is available from
the British Library

ISBN: 978-1-47213-863-7

Designed and typeset by Initial Typesetting Services, Edinburgh
Printed and bound in Great Britain by Clays Ltd, Elcograf S.p.A.

Papers used by Robinson are from well-managed forests
and other responsible sources

Robinson
An imprint of
Little, Brown Book Group
Carmelite House
50 Victoria Embankment
London EC4Y 0DZ

An Hachette UK Company
www.hachette.co.uk

www.littlebrown.co.uk

Contents

Part III:
What You Can Do to Help

Part IV:
Specific Types of Events

Preface

All children will encounter stressful experiences, and this might include loss and trauma.

Some children will take such experiences in their stride. There may be short-term changes in how they feel, think and act but then over time these reactions fade, and the children return, broadly speaking, to how they were before. The human body and mind are remarkably well designed to deal with difficult and stressful events.

Sadly though, for some children these losses and stresses are more difficult to adjust to and can overwhelm a child's ability to cope. As a result, some children continue to struggle, and develop lasting difficulties that interfere with their everyday lives.

Significant losses and trauma in childhood are more common than many people think. According to research in the UK in 2004, about 5 per cent of five to sixteen year olds had experienced the loss of a parent or sibling.[1] And in the US in 2020, 7 per cent of eighteen year olds had been bereaved of a parent or sibling.[2] Grief is a natural response to these losses. The child might experience an initial high level of distress but over time, as they adjust to their loss, their distress and difficulties ease. However, other bereaved children might respond differently, with intense difficulties that persist and worsen.

As far as trauma is concerned, research in England and Wales suggests that about a third of eighteen year olds have experienced 'death, threatened death, actual or threatened serious injury, or actual or threatened sexual violence',[3] (the definition of a traumatic event used by the American Psychiatric Association in describing Post-traumatic Stress Disorder – PTSD).[4] Similar studies have found rates of exposure to a similar potentially traumatic event as high as 68 per cent in the US.[5] Some of those children will have experienced multiple events. In addition to these relatively extreme events that clearly have the potential to be traumatic, there are other events that children experience which are not as extreme but are still so frightening or distressing that the event is experienced as traumatic and has a lasting negative impact on the child.

Stressful events are a bit like a psychological version of germs, bugs and diseases – some are an inevitable part of life. We can try to minimise exposure to the worst ones, but as we are unable to avoid all of them, it is preferable to help children to cope by boosting their immune system in advance and responding to whatever reactions they may have afterwards. It is the same for potentially traumatic events: we can try to minimise children's exposure to the worst ones, but some are unavoidable. Rather than trying to avoid absolutely every stressful event, it is helpful to maximise a child's ability to cope by providing the best possible environment for recovery.

In this book, I hope to help adults who are caring for children who have experienced all sorts of potentially traumatic or distressing events and bereavements. I will use a particular approach, known as the Cognitive Model of PTSD, to understand how very different events, including losses, impact children and what can be done to help. Research shows that this approach is helpful regardless of the type, the severity or the complexity of the events and the reactions of the child.[6] I will also draw on a couple of models that are specific to bereavement (Tasks of Mourning and Dual-processing Model of Grief).This will offer you a way of understanding how events can affect children, and importantly what you can do to help their recovery. Using this approach means that a child will be less likely to develop lasting difficulties because of the traumatic event or loss.

A practical evidence-based approach

This book is grounded in research and psychological theory. It will refer to research studies, and these will be listed at the end of the book so that you can follow them up in more detail if you wish. It also includes descriptions of some of the research studies; this is so that you can have some confidence that what I am suggesting has worked for many other children and families who might be having similar experiences to yours. I will use these studies to inform the practical suggestions about how you can help your child.

My own work as a clinical psychologist specialising in helping traumatised children and families is very firmly based on research. But ultimately, I am not an academic, I am a practitioner – someone who spends time with distressed and traumatised children and families, trying to puzzle out with them what can make things less bad. The suggestions in this book come as much from the families that I have worked with as they do from the research. And although there will be some very practical suggestions and examples, you know your child best, and you will know how and when to best use these suggestions.

How to use this book

You could read this book from its opening sentence through to the last word on the last page. But don't feel that you have to. Some parts of the book may not be relevant to you and your child. You can dip into the bits that look like they will be most useful – rather like choosing selected items from a buffet to make up a complete meal.

The book is split into five main parts. In Part 1, I will describe some of the different ways that bereavements and trauma can affect children and how you can start to notice and understand them. Some reactions are very common following traumatic events and loss, others less so. Part 1 will help you to know what to look out for so that you can consider what might be the most helpful kind of support. Part 1 also discusses the role of mental health diagnoses as they apply to children who have experienced losses or trauma. This might be useful if the child that you are caring for is involved with, or might need the help of, specialist mental health services.

In Part 2, I describe psychological approaches or models that can help explain the way that events might affect children, and what can be done to support them. This can vary a great deal between children. For example, twins may both experience the same traumatic event, and may both appear to be reacting in a similar way: difficulties sleeping, losing their temper more easily and lack of appetite. But the links between experiences and reactions may be different, with different implications for what would help. Accurately understanding what links the events to the reactions will enable you to provide the best help and support. I also describe some 'models of grief' that can help to understand how a bereavement can lead to certain grief reactions.

Part 3 describes what help and support is most likely to help children after loss or trauma, and explains how you as their carer are ideally placed to provide it. This may seem like the most important part of the book, but it relies very firmly on the earlier parts, so I wouldn't recommend going straight to Part 3.

Part 4 will consider different types of events and losses, and offers some specific practical ideas to consider.

Finally in Part 5, I turn my attention to you! When children are affected by loss or trauma, it can of course have a significant impact on the parents and carers too. When helping your child with loss and trauma it can be easy to forget your own needs. I will be very strongly encouraging you to look after yourself so that you are in the best position possible to look after your child.

PART I

◇◇◇◇◇◇◇◇◇◇◇◇

Understanding Your Child's Reactions to Loss and Trauma

Sadly, loss and trauma are a more common experience for children than we would wish. When we talk about 'loss' for the purpose of this book, we are referring to the experience that a child has when they have been bereaved because someone they know has died. And when we talk about 'trauma', we don't mean a difficult or stressful experience that might cause some distress or difficulties for a short while. We mean adverse events that are intense enough or severe enough that they risk causing lasting distress or enduring difficulties. These could include:

- Individual events (such as abuse, bullying, assaults, accidents, illnesses or medical interventions)

- Natural events (such as storms or floods)

- Large-scale events (such as terrorist attacks, pandemics or wars)

In this part of the book, I will discuss some of the ways that children react to loss and trauma, which will hopefully help you to identify your child's reactions. The following parts will then help you to understand what is happening, what you can do to help their recovery, and if they need any additional support.

The book focuses on children aged from five to twelve years old, but is relevant for children and young people of any age. You will be able to adapt the approaches suggested to suit the young person or child you are supporting by taking into account how independent they are, how much help they generally feel comfortable with, and their level of understanding. Of course, children can react in very many different ways regardless of their age. I cannot hope to cover every possible reaction but there are some that are more common and some that are more concerning.

Different reactions

Immediately after, or even during, very stressful or traumatic events and bereavements children may of course be distressed. Distress, upset, anxiety, fear and other difficulties may be unavoidable and perfectly understandable. Such reactions, even when quite extreme, are not always a cause for concern. For many children, their reactions will subside over time and life will return to normal or settle to a new normal.

Research suggests that typical reactions to potentially traumatic events generally follow one of four paths:[7]

- Unaffected: The child does not experience difficulties

- Recovered: Difficulties directly after the event but these diminish over time

- Delayed: The child seems to be unaffected to begin with but later on difficulties emerge

- Lasting: Difficulties directly after the event that persist over time

These four patterns are illustrated graphically below:

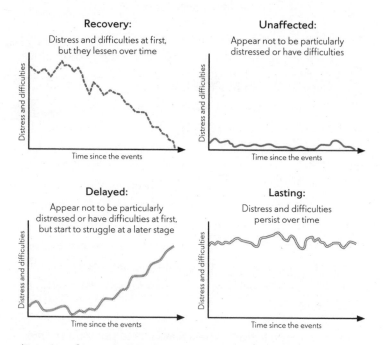

Recovery:
Distress and difficulties at first, but they lessen over time

Unaffected:
Appear not to be particularly distressed or have difficulties

Delayed:
Appear not to be particularly distressed or have difficulties at first, but start to struggle at a later stage

Lasting:
Distress and difficulties persist over time

(Based on the work of Professor George Bonanno, 2004.)

It's really difficult to be exact about the timescale because different losses and traumas will affect different children in very different ways. Regardless of how long since the loss or the trauma, this book is about how to help children to get onto the recovery path.

One way of describing children's distress and difficulties after traumatic events or bereavements is to think about the symptoms of Post-traumatic Stress Disorder or PTSD. Since the four paths above were first described there have been several studies that measure symptoms of PTSD at different time points following potentially traumatic events. These studies have consistently found that:

- Many children (sometimes over half) appear to be relatively *unaffected* and do not report many difficulties

- Some (often about a third) follow the *recovery* path. They are very distressed for a few days or weeks after the event but a few months later their distress is much less

- The remainder (often about 10 per cent to 20 per cent) have problems at the beginning that do not improve (*lasting*), or they seem to be OK at first but then develop difficulties later on (*delayed*).

For example, Professor Alisic and colleagues reviewed forty-two different research studies, which between them assessed nearly 3,500 children who had experienced potentially traumatic events. They found that on average, only about 16 per cent developed PTSD, and would therefore be considered to be following the 'enduring' path.[8] Of course, PTSD is not the only problem that can result from traumatic events and there are plenty of other adverse ways that children might react to events. However, this study is one example that shows that only a proportion of children who experience potentially traumatic events will actually develop lasting difficulties.

We also know that many children who initially have high levels of distress and difficulties, will make a good recovery even without any specialist help or support, and will follow the 'recovery' path. For example, Professor Rachel Hiller together with colleagues, analysed eighteen different pieces of research and found that nearly a quarter of children with PTSD one month after the events, did *not* have PTSD three months after the events. And of those children that still had PTSD three months after the events, a quarter of them no longer had PTSD six months after the events.[9]

It seems that there are some things that are consistently linked with lasting difficulties. Obviously the more severe or the more frightening an experience is, the more *likely* a child will struggle. But interestingly, the severity of the event actually only makes a small difference to how likely it is a child will have difficulties. Lack of social support, families not working well together, trying to avoid thinking about what has happened, and other stressors (e.g. moving school or a change in family circumstances) are all related to lasting difficulties. Probably the most important factor that predicts how children will manage after traumatic events and bereavements is the meaning that they make of the event – how does their experience colour the way they see themselves, other people and the world in general? It is difficult to study accurately how different events directly affect a person's mental health more generally and in the longer term. And this can be particularly complicated if they have experienced several potentially traumatic events or bereavements during their childhood. But we do know from a large body of research that experiencing traumatic events in childhood increases the risk of developing mental health difficulties in the future.[10]

Even on the 'recovery' path described above (where distress and difficulties decrease over time) the recovery rarely happens smoothly. It will fluctuate and at times it might seem that things are worse than at the beginning, despite improving overall. Sometimes there can be temporary setbacks or increases in difficulties and distress triggered by specific events that happen after the actual traumatic events, such as funerals, enquiries, criminal trials, moving home, etc. Such temporary increases in difficulties are understandable, so if that's what seems to be happening with your child, don't assume that things are going backwards or getting permanently worse.

Part 2 will help you to understand how trauma or loss affect children, and Part 3 will help you to think about how to create the environment around your child that will maximise their opportunities for recovery. But first I'm going to focus on how children react to loss and trauma so that you will have a better idea of what to look out for.

Noticing the reactions of your child

Some reactions in children are easily noticed by those around them (e.g. if they are getting into fights, having frightening nightmares, or refusing to leave their carer). Other reactions may not be so obviously linked to events. For example, nightmares about the actual events are obviously linked, but frightening dreams that do not replay the event may still be a reaction. And there may be other reactions that you and others around your child are not even aware of. So, it's important for you and the other adults around your child to be aware of any changes, and to consider if they may be related to their trauma or loss.

Children may not mention their reactions and worries to the adults around them. They might hope that the reactions will just go away, or perhaps feel embarrassed by them; they might worry that they will be told not to be so silly, or that talking about their fears might make them worse. Some children try to protect their carers by not mentioning their reactions to them. For example, when I ask them in front of their carers, many children that I have worked with do not mention their nightmares, but when I see them on their own, they tell me that they are having frequent frightening dreams. When I have gently asked why they did not say they were getting nightmares when their carer was in the room, they have explained that when they talk about their nightmares, their carer gets really upset and anxious, so they have stopped mentioning them in front of them.

This clinical experience is supported by research. Professor Eva Alisic and colleagues reviewed a number of studies in this area, and found that carers were often not aware of the severity of their children's reactions. When children themselves were asked about their experience, instead of asking their carers, three times as many children were diagnosed with PTSD.[11] And of course many parents and carers find it really upsetting to see that their child is struggling and so they may understandably prefer to minimise the difficulties or even try to avoid them completely.

It is therefore important to ask your child specifically about their reactions. They may not be able to initiate a conversation about their problems but might be able to respond to your gentle direct questions – they may even be relieved that you asked, and they no longer have to suffer in silence on their own. Later in this book there is a section entitled 'How to Talk to Your Child About Their Reactions' where I will suggest some ideas about how to start these conversations. Before moving on to this, let's first consider some reactions you might notice. Remember though, many children will have some difficulties after traumatic events or bereavements – that doesn't mean that there is necessarily a problem that needs specialist help. Following the advice later in this book will improve their chances of recovering over time and will also help you to know when to seek additional support.

Key points

- Different children will react differently to loss and trauma.

- Many reactions are very natural and understandable.

- Research suggests that typical reactions to potentially traumatic events and losses could be described as following one of a number of particular paths: Unaffected, Recovery, Delayed or Lasting.

- The approach in this book can help you identify the difficulties your child might be experiencing, and provide practical, evidence-based guidance on how you can help them recover.

2

Identifying Problems

Below I identify some of the difficulties that children may have with adjusting to traumatic events or bereavement. In the next chapter, there is a checklist for you to use to identify if your child is experiencing any of these problems.

1) Intrusive Memories

In Chapter 2, I will explain in more detail how traumatic memories are different to other memories. But briefly, memories for traumatic events tend to be:

- **Volatile:** Unlike other memories that might be quite hard to recall, traumatic memories are triggered incredibly easily, they may even seem like they come out of nowhere.

- **Vivid:** Traumatic memories consist of the 'data' of the event – the sounds, sights, tastes, touches, smells, thoughts and feelings, instead of the story of events. The traumatic memories may be so intense that it actually feels as if the events are happening again.

- **Fragmented:** Rather than having an account of the whole event from beginning through to the end, traumatic memories tend to be stored as individual fragments or moments, possibly the worst moments.

- **Distressing:** when the memory is triggered, the original distress of the time may also be triggered.

This means that your child may feel as if they are re-experiencing the actual events rather than simply recalling the memories. This can be very frightening for children: the events themselves may make children believe that they have no control over what happens around them, and then the uncontrollable nature of the memory can make them believe that they have no control over what happens inside their own minds! For example, children who have been bereaved may experience intrusive memories of the way the person died, or even the way that they *imagine* they died.

Having nightmares

Many children will start to have bad dreams after traumatic events or bereavements. They may wake up very distressed, and they may not be able, or may not want to, recall exactly what was happening in the dream. The dreams may very clearly involve reliving moments of traumatic events, or they may only relate indirectly to the events (e.g. a child who has been physically abused may have more general dreams about being chased and not being able to get away). It may be difficult to identify the link between the dreams and the events, other than the emotions that they prompt.

Re-experiencing sensations (images, smells, sounds, tastes, touches) related to the events

Traumatic memories are often very easily triggered and may be stored more as sensory information of the event than the story (more on this in Chapter 2). So children may re-experience the particular physical or emotional reactions that they had at the time, rather than remember a narrative account.

Examples of traumatic memories

Nina (aged 6) had a history of domestic violence with her stepfather being violent and shouting at both her and her mother. She described to me how she could still hear her stepfather's voice shouting at her, even though she knew that he was in prison.

Luka (aged 10) whose family home had been in a fire, had to stop drawing the picture of his trauma, because when he got to the point where the fire started, he was absolutely sure that he could smell smoke, so he insisted that we set off the fire alarm and all leave the building.

Aisha (aged 8) was in the front seat of the car when it crashed into an oncoming lorry. She vividly remembered the blood 'pouring' out of her side, she described it as being 'like a tap'. When I first met her, she described how she would often re-experience the sensation of warm

---

liquid flowing down her leg, and it would often occur with no apparent trigger.

These examples show how the memories can often be very sensory rather than verbal.

Flashbacks – acting or feeling as if it is happening again

A flashback is an extreme form of intrusive memory. The memory is so vivid and intense that the person experiencing it believes that the events are actually happening again. It is so immersive that they lose touch with the 'here and now' because they are so in touch with the 'there and then'. This can be extremely frightening, and the child may feel that there is something wrong with them. Flashbacks may be triggered by something in the environment, but the child may not be aware of the trigger. For example, a child who has been physically abused by an angry adult male in the family home may have flashbacks that are triggered by a male teacher who raises his voice to make himself heard above the hubbub of the classroom.

Having thoughts about the events that intrude into their minds or keep going round and round

Some children are preoccupied with thinking about the events. Thoughts about what happened, why it happened, and how it happened, keep coming into their minds or keep circling around in their minds. The child may be:

- Constantly thinking about or remembering the events

- Mulling over events to try to make sense of them

- Worrying about the future because of the impact the events have had on their view of the world and their future

This type of preoccupation or rumination may be unhelpful, because although they are at least thinking things through rather than avoiding them, it can be in quite a 'stuck' way that is not realistic or helpful. Often it involves going over and over the worst moments of the event, or confirming an unhelpful and unrealistic perception, rather than thinking it through in a more balanced way. For example, eight-year-old Seb thought it was his fault that he was run over by a car, and he kept thinking about the fact that it was his fault. This thought was so upsetting that he tried to push it out of his head. But it kept coming back. This meant that until he came to therapy, he didn't have the chance to think things through more completely and in a more balanced way so that he could 'recalibrate' the way that he assigned responsibility.

Repeatedly playing back particular parts of the events, or themes related to them

Some children will start to re-enact the events through their play or drawings. Or they may start to act out specific themes of the events, if not the event itself. For example, if they have been physically abused, they may start to play a bigger cuddly toy stamping on a smaller one. Play is one of the ways in which children make sense of the world, so it is no surprise to see elements of the traumatic events 'leaking' into their play-world. Indeed, this may be extremely useful. For example, during the Covid pandemic, many children played out themes of being ill, staying at home and missing school. But if this trauma-based play continues to happen even some time after the events, it may be an indication that things have become a bit stuck, and they have not been able to process the memories and make sense of the events.

Suddenly or repeatedly talking about the traumatic events

Some children will suddenly start talking about what happened, maybe when you least expect it, maybe at very inconvenient moments. For example, when her mother went shopping with her, six-year-old Farah insisted on telling the people working in shops about her traumatic bereavement. It was as if she couldn't help herself. Other children keep going over and over the same part of the memory. It would be like a social media site repeating the same short clip from a video when you actually want to watch the whole thing, and even when you try to play a completely different video, it replays that same clip.

So, rather than telling the whole story from start to finish, they keep repeating a particular aspect of the events, perhaps the most frightening moments. For example, they might keep talking about the moment that they heard people screaming.

Experiencing intense reactions to reminders

Sometimes children can experience strong psychological or physiological reactions to reminders without other aspects of the memory being triggered. For example, a child who was abused at a young age by someone wearing a particular aftershave might catch a waft of a similar aftershave when walking down the street and, without explicitly recalling the abuse, they may find that they have a panic attack or are frozen with fear. It's as if their brains do not remember the events, but their bodies do. If children do not realise why their bodies are reacting like that, it can be terrifying, because it may feel like they have no control over their own body, let alone what goes on around them.

2) Avoidance

The memories of the events, or the meaning that they make of the events, can be so distressing that children may invest lots of energy in avoiding anything that could possibly trigger memories or thoughts about the events. Sometimes children are so good at avoidance, that it can look as if everything is fine.

Trying not to talk about the events

They may not want to talk about it and will avoid conversations about it; this avoidance can be quite extreme and widespread. For instance, if a child's father died in a car crash, they may avoid any conversation about their father, even if the conversation is about some pleasant aspect of their time with their father. The memory of the way that he died may be so volatile that it is triggered by anything related to their father, even pleasant memories.

Trying to avoid people, activities or places that might remind them or cause them to think about the events

In order to avoid remembering or thinking about the events, children may start to avoid people, activities or places that could be linked to the events. This could also become more generalised – for example, they may start to avoid any crowded place, and not just a specific location, because the experience of crowds triggers their memories.

Being reluctant to go to bed or sleep

Perhaps because of the fear of bad dreams, or because of thoughts and memories that intrude when there are fewer distractions such as the time between going to bed and going to sleep, some children are extremely reluctant to go to bed, or they may simply refuse to do so. They might learn that if they cause enough trouble at bedtime, an adult will come to them, even if just to tell them off. For a traumatised child, having an adult there to tell you off might be preferable to being left on your own with your worries, thoughts, memories or nightmares. Even if the child does make it to bed, they may do everything they can to try to stay awake rather than go to sleep to avoid nightmares. I have worked with a number of children who play games on their phone in an attempt to prevent themselves from going to sleep. But then eventually in the early hours of the morning they fall asleep out of sheer exhaustion. Some children insist on sleeping with their carer, or that their carer remains with them. Some children know that their carer will not let them into their beds and so the children wait until they know their carer is asleep and then creep into their bed without their carer even noticing.

Keeping their minds busy with other things

Children might invest significant effort in trying to prevent the memories and thoughts from intruding, desperately trying to fill their minds with other things. This may work in the short term, but the thoughts and the memories will often find a way back in when they are less able to fill their minds with other content to block out the memories.

3) Physiological Hyperarousal – the fight-flight-freeze response

Here, we are talking about the way that following some events, children find themselves in a state of alert and readiness that is ongoing and does not pass.

When children are startled, frightened or stressed by events, their stress response system leaps into action. Various systems within their brains and their bodies work together in an incredibly complicated way to react to the trigger and get them ready to deal with the perceived threat. This is sometimes called the 'fight-flight-freeze' response because it prepares us to fight, or to run away (flee), or to keep really still and avoid being hurt (freeze). This is usually not a conscious decision – that would take too long. The brain and the body work together, bypassing some of the more 'thoughtful' and reflective routes within the brain. There may not be time to consider the event carefully and weigh up the pros and cons of different actions, so the brain and body respond almost instantly and automatically – too quickly for the child even to realise what is going on. For example, if you are standing close to a road and a very loud motorbike roars past, you may find that you have stepped back from the road automatically, without making a conscious decision to do so. Then, either when the perceived threat has passed, or when the more rational parts of the brain catch up and realise that it is not actually a threat, the system 'resets' and returns to the resting state.

Something as harmless as a balloon popping unexpectedly may cause a child to experience quite an intense physiological reaction. This would be quite a useful response if in fact the noise was a gunshot in which case running away very quickly would be a really useful thing to do. So, the body reacts just in case it is a threat. But when the child realises that it is just a balloon and is harmless, then their body's response system 'resets' and gradually returns to a state of rest. This process can be assisted by the adults around them, and particularly those that they know and trust, reassuring them and perhaps offering some physical comfort so that they can be sure that they are safe.

 This is a bit like a set of kitchen scales. It starts at zero, and when you put a weight on it, the indicator moves in response to the weight. When the weight is taken off, the indicator returns to zero. In a similar way, we may start in a 'resting state' but when we perceive that something unexpected or threatening is happening, our minds and bodies react instantly and we experience a higher state of arousal. When the event is over, and the threat has passed then our minds and bodies return to their resting state.

But if you put a weight on the scales that is too heavy for it, it might affect the adjustment, so when you take the weight off, the indicator does not return to zero. Similarly, when a child experiences an event that is *traumatic* rather than just *stressful*, their stress response system may struggle to reset and return to its resting state. They remain on a higher state of alert so they may become more sensitive to future triggers.

This persistent hyperarousal is responsible for a number of the difficulties and problems that children have following loss and traumatic events. Some children will be constantly on a higher level of alert and readiness, some will have a much lower threshold for what is perceived as a possible threat, some will react more quickly, and some will react more extremely. Such reactions may be quite appropri-ate and even useful in an environment where an actual threat is ongoing. The hyperarousal may be a way that someone's body adapts quite helpfully to a genuine ongoing threat. For example, if a child lives in a house where domestic violence is common, it could be really useful to be constantly on the lookout for possible violence and to be constantly ready to act. But it might be unnecessary and even problematic to be constantly on alert when the threat has passed, and the child is in fact safe. The difficulty is that even if the child 'knows' that they are now safe, the parts of the brain responsible for reacting quickly to possible threats may override that knowledge 'just in case'. It would be like having a smoke detector that was once so overwhelmed by lots of thick smoke, that its smoke sensor is now over-sensitive and it gets set off far too easily. In 1996, Daniel Goleman called this the 'amygdala hijack';[12] the amygdala is a part of the brain that is central in the reaction to stress and threat, and this reaction takes over, deliberately preventing a more considered response.

There are lots of ways in which this hyperarousal affects children, including:

Having difficulties in getting to sleep, or staying asleep

Even without the intrusive thoughts and memories mentioned earlier, children that are in a constant state of readiness and arousal will obviously find it difficult to sleep. Their bodies are ready for *action* – not ready for *inaction* and rest. And at night-time, when most other people are asleep, noises may appear louder, and there are fewer distractions so it is easier for children's minds to wander

– either back to the traumatic events, or to start to imagine what might happen next. If they are able to get to sleep, it may be a very light sleep and they may wake up during the night, possibly many times.

Having night terrors

Night terrors are different to nightmares. In night terrors, the child rarely wakes up, but is extremely distressed while asleep. They may cry, scream and even flail around without actually waking up. Night terrors are incredibly distressing for those around the children, but when they wake up, the children are usually fine and have no memory of the distress.

Sleep walking

I have worked with several children who have started to sleepwalk following traumatic events. It's as if their bodies are in a state of arousal intended for action, and therefore simply unable to relax – even when they are asleep. Their ongoing stress response is readying them for action rather than helping them to relax and sleep.

Being irritable, losing temper easily, anger or violence

The ongoing hyperarousal described earlier may mean that children are more irritable than they would have been. They may lose their temper more quickly and more extremely because their default or resting arousal level is several notches higher than other children, so it takes less to trigger an angry outburst and their outbursts tend to be more severe.

Sometimes children get misunderstood as oppositional or violent, when in fact they are scared and reacting automatically to something that they perceived to be threatening. The adults around them may not understand this, because they cannot see what it was that triggered the outburst.

For example, if teachers are not aware of a child's history (or don't have the time or motivation to take such things into consideration), then they may misunderstand a child's behaviour. They may respond to what they see as a 'noncompliant' child by being assertive and enforcing clear boundaries. But the child may already be in a highly aroused state and unable to see the teacher's response for what it is. And if the child has a history of domestic abuse, they may be highly attuned to angry adults, so if they perceive the teacher as being angry, the child's reaction may be automatic and extreme. As described earlier, their amygdala – a part of the brain that is central to the stress response – sounds the alarm and their body is quickly made ready for action: an amygdala hijack. In turn, this may provoke a stronger response from the teacher. It is easy to see how this can lead to a vicious cycle which can cause significant problems. That's not to say that traumatised children should be given a licence to behave as they wish, but some understanding by the adults around a child of how they may be triggered can be invaluable in helping the child to stay calmer.

Being jumpy, easily startled

Similarly, because of this raised level of arousal, some children are more easily startled. And once startled it may take much longer for them to settle again. For example, lots of children may jump when the first very loud firework goes off at the beginning of a fireworks display, even though they were waiting for the display to start. Their heart rates may increase, they may shriek and even shake. But shortly after, they will relax, their arousal systems will go back to rest, and they will be able to enjoy the display. Subsequent loud fireworks will likely lead to a milder reaction. But a child who has been traumatised and is now operating on a higher level of arousal, might have a more intense reaction to the first firework, they might remain startled by that first firework for much longer. They might jump just as much to each subsequent firework rather than getting used to them. Even when they get home, they may not feel like eating or sleeping because their startle response is still active.

Freezing in response to perceived threats

Sometimes, children's anxiety freezes them to the spot rather than readying them to act. Maybe this has some root in evolution, if a predator comes along that is too big to fight and too fast to run from, then maybe being really still in the hope that it doesn't notice you is actually a very good survival strategy. The child whose anxiety makes them run off, or lash out, can be quite easy to spot, but sometimes children who freeze may go unnoticed. But that automatic physical response can be quite frightening for children and confusing for those around them.

Being hypervigilant and having concentration problems

Following certain experiences, children may be hypervigilant and always on the lookout, frequently looking around them. This makes sense from a survival point of view because if they believe that the world is unsafe or unpredictable or that they are vulnerable, then being more alert to what is going around could be very useful. But it may be unhelpful when there is no actual threat. Such children may be so busy paying attention to *everything* around them to work out if it is a threat or not that they struggle to concentrate on the things that others think they should be paying attention to. For example, in a classroom, it is unlikely that the whiteboard on which the teacher is writing, or the book in front of them, is going to be a threat, so from a survival point of view why pay attention to that? But what about that noise in the corridor, or that person walking past the window, or the children whispering behind them? In the minds of traumatised children, any of those could be a potential threat, so it makes good sense to pay attention to them. Sometimes this hypervigilance is mistaken by those around the child as an inability to pay attention, and this may lead to an inaccurate understanding (e.g. of Attention Deficit Hyperactivity Disorder, ADHD). This in turn could lead to the wrong intervention being offered. It is not that the child is *unable* to pay attention to something, in fact they may be very good at paying attention – just not to the things that everyone else wants them to.

Being overly sensitive to sensory stimulation

Being more alert to everything going on around them, might mean that children become hyper-sensitive to all sorts of sensory stimulation. For example, they might start to get very upset when they are in noisy environments like playgrounds or shopping centres; they might start to hate the sensation of certain materials or the labels in their clothes; they might prefer soft lights, or find that they can't cope with strong smells or tastes. This sensitivity might then have a broader impact, as they may start to avoid particular situations or become more wary of things that previously they were not worried about.

All these states of hyperarousal can lead to physical reactions such as changes to appetite and headaches, especially if the reaction goes on for some time. I will discuss these types of physical reactions below as they may also happen due to anxiety.

4) Anxiety

Following certain events, children might be a little bit more sensitive and careful, for example if they were playing with a dog that got over-excited, barked loudly and maybe even snapped at them, they might become anxious when they next see a dog as they worry about whether it will also snap at them. But, as they come into contact with more dogs that do not snap at them, they may start to feel more confident around dogs again. However, some children become very anxious after certain events and their anxiety does not decrease spontaneously. In the example above with the dog, they might then start to avoid all dogs, even TV programmes with dogs. They might refuse to go to the playground in the local park just in case there are dogs

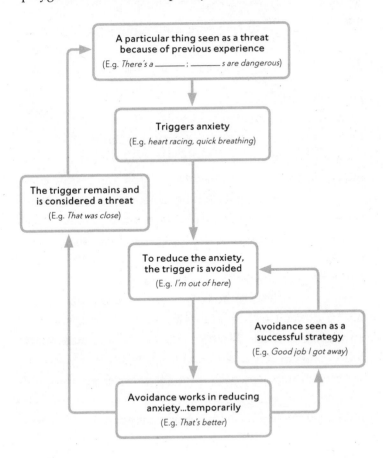

there and if they ever spot a dog they may go off in the opposite direction. Such avoidance might help to decrease their anxiety in the short term, and therefore they might consider this to be a successful strategy. But in fact, they never get to learn that most dogs do not snap.

In the next chapter, I will explain in detail how some events change the way that children see themselves, others, and the world in general. And how this makes them feel anxious and insecure.

Being reluctant to leave carers and clingy

Following traumatic events or bereavements, some children develop separation anxiety and are reluctant to leave their main carers. At times of stress or threat, it is quite usual and healthy for children to seek out their carers, they might want to stay with their carers more for a while after the events. They might be a little more anxious about separating from their carers for a few days, or even weeks. They might simply need the additional reassurance that comes from being closer to their carers for a while until they rediscover their confidence. However, some children continue to experience anxiety for much longer. These children might find it difficult to leave their carers and perhaps find it impossible to return to school. Staying close to their carers relieves the anxiety in the short term, and so is very effective. Some carers may be anxious themselves, and therefore may actively encourage their children to stay nearby. But ultimately that strategy can become extremely problematic.

Having new fears

After traumatic events or bereavements, children might develop new fears that they did not have before. For example, some children might become afraid of the dark, having previously not been. They might be afraid that a mild headache is a brain tumour. It's as if the events have made them just too good at being afraid – they see more things as potentially threatening, they overestimate the threat posed by things, they over-react to potential threats and they find it more difficult to calm down.

Feeling panicky

Some children can start to feel very anxious quite suddenly and may not even know why. They may have physical feelings such as increased heart rate, fast shallow breathing, tingling sensations, shakiness, feeling sick or feeling faint. When a child panics, they could interpret these signs of anxiety as being dangerous, and this then increases their anxiety. As noted above, it's as if the traumatic events or the bereavement has made them very good at anxiety, and this ability now takes on a life of its own.

Losing confidence

Some traumatised or bereaved children lose their confidence. Perhaps they now feel that things are very unpredictable or that bad things will always happen, so they don't want to risk it. They might stop giving new things a try, and perhaps become overly shy, even in situations when they would have previously been quite confident.

Feeling generally worried

For some children, worry becomes their default emotional state. So they don't only get very anxious about specific triggers, they just feel a general sense of dread most of the time. They might struggle to know what it really is that they are anxious about, but they just know that they are anxious.

Having obsessions and compulsions, having to check that they have done certain things

In the face of events over which children feel they have no control, some start to latch on to behaviours that make them *feel as if* they have some control. They might start to repeat certain actions or rituals again and again. This gives them the illusion of having some control, which might in the short term be quite reassuring. But this can become a habit, and they could then start to feel anxious if they do not perform that specific action or ritual, and they start to feel a strong compulsion to do it in order to reduce their anxiety. This might be particularly true if children believe that they are in some way responsible for the events. They might think that if only they had done something different the bad things would not have happened. They then start to do various things in the hope that it will prevent more bad things happening.

Suffering from headaches, tummy aches, and other physical symptoms

Worry and anxiety obviously have something of a physical component, so it is no surprise that many children and young people who worry have lots of headaches, or tummy aches or other physical symptoms. Sometimes the children and those around them might not realise that they are linked to the worry. Sometimes children who worry, notice their bodily sensations more and as they focus on them, they feel as if they are getting worse.

Having a change in appetite

Some children who are worried, anxious or afraid lots of the time have no appetite. It's as if they are so consumed with their worry that they don't have the motivation to consume food. It might be because of the hormones associated with anxiety that turn off their appetite, or it might be that the physical sensations of anxiety (such as feeling sick) make them not want to eat. Others might find some short-term comfort from eating, but because it's only short-term, they find themselves eating more and more in order to try to relieve their distress, and this overeating can become problematic.

5) Dissociation – feeling numb and disconnected

Some children react to events with what seems like the opposite to over-arousal. Rather than being hyper-aware of everything that is going on around them and inside them, they seem to block off information, thoughts, feelings or memories. They may feel emotionally numb, and they may feel disconnected from their surroundings or even from their own bodies. Sometimes this can be difficult to spot in children because there might be no obvious signs on the outside of what is happening inside their minds and bodies. Although it isn't a very well understood term, this is sometimes called dissociation. In the book *Harry Potter and the Goblet of Fire* by J.K. Rowling, Harry Potter seemed to dissociate after Lord Voldemort tried to kill him. Even when Harry is back in the safety of his school, Hogwarts, and with people that he knows, loves and trusts, he feels numb and unreal.

Dissociation may be quite a useful strategy for dealing with extremely traumatic situations from which the child could not escape. But if they continue to dissociate after the events have ended, perhaps in response to stressful (but not traumatic) events, or in response to reminders of the traumatic events, it can cause significant difficulties. When children dissociate, they might feel detached from themselves, or they might feel as if they are in a dream or experience a sense of unreality. This obviously is likely to affect their ability to learn and their ability to interact with others. From the outside, it might look as though children who are dissociating are just daydreaming. But, unlike daydreaming, dissociation is an automatic process in response to stress and involves an altered sense of perception.

These sorts of reactions are sometimes referred to as dereal-isation (feeling as if things are not real) or depersonalisation (feeling a difference in self-awareness and possibly feeling detached from oneself).

The following are some signs of dissociation:

- Appearing spaced out or in a daze

- Forgetting things easily

- Not remembering what they were doing for periods of time

- Losing track of time

- Feeling detached from themself (e.g. referring to themself as 'he' or 'she')

- Daydreaming

- Blanking out when stressed

- Feeling emotionally numb (i.e. seeming flat or as if they don't have the normal range of emotions)

It's difficult enough for adults to be able to notice and describe these sorts of reactions in themselves, so obviously it is even more difficult for children to be able to describe them. Therefore, it's particularly important that adults around the children are aware of them. Some children might be suffering with some of these subtle reactions, but they can appear to be doing quite well. However, a certain amount of daydreaming and forgetfulness is perfectly normal in children (and adults). If you do notice these things in your children, ask yourself whether this is 'new' or whether they were always a bit like that, and whether it's actually causing a problem. It can be helpful to ask other adults that know them (e.g. teachers, childminders, extended family) whether they have noticed any changes.

6) Other changes in thoughts and feelings

Having inaccurate thoughts about the consequences of the events

Some children over-estimate the impact of events; for example, they see themselves as permanently damaged, or think that they will never be able to do certain things again. This makes them less prepared to try things, which then just confirms their belief that they can't manage things.

It is helpful, if possible, to explore with your child what understanding they have of any reactions. For example, asking them why do they think they are finding it diffi-cult to sleep? Do they think that they will never be able to sleep properly again? Do they see this as a sign that they are now permanently changed from how they were before the event?

Developing omen formation

Children sometimes declare that they knew an event was going to happen in advance. This is called 'omen formation'. Perhaps this is a way of trying to see the world as a little less unpredictable and therefore a little less scary. But such thoughts often lead to the child feeling very guilty because they think that if they knew it was going to happen, they should have done something to stop it from happening.

Feeling very sad, much of the time

A lot of the research on children after potentially traumatic events has focused on reactions and symptoms associated with Post-traumatic Stress Disorder (PTSD). But there is also plenty of evidence that many children will react to traumatic events by feeling persistently unhappy (sometimes known as depression). In fact, some research indicates that after a traumatic event depression is more often a problem than PTSD.[13]

If a traumatic event changes a child's view of themselves, and they start to believe that no one likes them and that they are useless, this might result in them thinking that there is no point in going out, and that their friends don't really want them there. These thoughts may make them feel sad and low, which in turn makes them feel lethargic, and this all combines to make them avoid going out. Not going out results in friends and families no longer bothering to invite them out, which in turn makes them feel increasingly isolated and depressed, and also simply confirms their beliefs that no one likes them.

In the next chapter of the book, I will 'map out' how traumatic events and bereavements can lead to a child becoming depressed and isolated and how those difficulties are maintained by their avoidance.

This is different to the perfectly natural sadness that a child might feel after somebody has died. Often after a bereavement children will understandably feel sad, but they have happier moments as well, the sadness is not pervasive, and following a loss, children might jump in and out of their sadness. Depression is about a more persistent sadness that permeates most things most of the time.

The signs of low self-esteem and depression can sometimes be difficult to spot as the child may keep their thoughts to themselves, but there may be some clues in what they do and say. For example:

- They may stop giving things a go (such as answering questions in class, trying out new activities) because they are afraid that they will fail.

- They may find it difficult to enjoy anything.

- They may lack motivation to do things, even things that they used to enjoy.

- They may see everything in a very negative way and have little ability to see the positive side of things (even twisting and distorting positive things to fit with their negative feelings).

- They may lose their appetite or over-eat.

- They may start to think more about death and even feel as if they want to die.

- They may start to sleep much longer.

7) Other reactions

Feeling Guilty

Some children will feel guilty. They might feel guilty that others have experienced worse things than them, or guilty if they believe that they had a role in the trauma or believe they could have stopped it. Or they feel guilty because they are able to still feel happy sometimes.

Regressing

Regression is when a child behaves in a younger way, one that you thought they had grown out of. Some children might seem to regress or lose some of their developmental skills following stressful or frightening events. For example, they start to wet the bed again having been dry at nights, or they suddenly need their cuddly toys around them having previously outgrown them. For many this will be a temporary stage, but for others it may continue for weeks and is a sign of the toll that events have taken on them.

Parentification

In an attempt to take control of things, or to try to make up for any guilt they feel, some children become 'parentified', that is that they start to take on the role of the carer, perhaps for their siblings or even for the parents.

Amnesia – being unable to remember significant parts of the event

Occasionally, children are unable to recall important aspects of their traumatic experiences. This is different to avoidance – avoidance is when children deliberately make an effort to avoid thinking about or being reminded about events. Amnesia is when children are *unable* to recall the memory even if they try. There may be small or large portions of the memory that they simply cannot recall. For some children, being unable to recall parts of the event can be a great relief to them. Other children find it very frightening that they cannot remember something. They might worry about what actually happened, and worry that they are permanently damaged in some way. The missing bits of memories sometimes return over time, but not always.

Sara's amnesia

Nine-year-old Sara had no memory at all of what happened from 9.00am until 1.00pm on the day of her traumatic event. She remembered walking along the pavement with her uncle, going to the post office. The next thing she remembered was sitting in the hospital with her mother. She was told that a car had lost control, had come onto the pavement, crashed into her uncle, and that she had phoned for an ambulance then phoned her mother; her uncle had been taken to hospital in an ambulance and her mother had taken her to the hospital in her car. She could not remember any of those details. At first, she was very worried by this amnesia but when she found out that this was simply her reaction to the trauma, she felt very reassured. Six months later, the actual memory had not returned, but she was no longer worried about it.

Taking longer for emotions to pass

Children might not necessarily react more easily, more quickly or more severely, but you may notice that they just take longer to recover their emotional balance after their emotions have been triggered. So, after losing their temper, getting worried or being sad, rather than regaining their emotional balance, you might find they get 'stuck' in their emotions.

Having problems at school

In some ways, a good school can provide the ideal post-trauma or post-bereavement environment, with its structure, routines, predictability, adults that are familiar, trusted and concerned, and social support from peers. However, traumatised or bereaved children might not make ideal students!

Even if the various elements of the school environment might be useful, the children are simply not set up to learn. As discussed above, they may be good at concentrating on anything that they perceive as a risk, but not so good at concentrating on their schoolwork. They may be suffering from intrusive memories or working hard to avoid them. They may be finding loud playgrounds and busy class-rooms very anxiety provoking. Because they are constantly on the lookout and wound up, it may not take much to push them over the edge, resulting in frequent temper tantrums

Taking risks

Sometimes, following traumatic events or loss, children start to take more risks. Perhaps because they are now operating on a much higher physiological base-line level, they have to do something more extreme in order to feel any impact. Or the events or loss might have made them care less about whether they live or die, so they are less concerned about the risks.

Deliberately hurting themselves

Some children find the reactions listed above so difficult to deal with that they start to hurt themselves as a way to provide some sort of relief from their other difficulties. They might start to cut themselves, bang their heads, slap their face, etc. Although painful, it does mean that temporarily they can focus on something else rather than their difficulties, and they might prefer to have a pain that they are in control of, rather than other difficulties over which they feel they have no control.

Key points

- Children can have a range of difficulties in adjusting to traumatic events or bereavement.

- This chapter has described some of these difficulties, and what can keep them going.

- Difficulties can include having intrusive memories, avoiding things that could trigger memories or thoughts of the event, being in a constant state of alert and readiness, anxiety, feeling numb and disconnected, as well as other changes in thoughts, feelings and behaviours.

- Knowing more about the range of difficulties that a child might experience can help you spot them so you can take action.

3

Recognising Your Child's Reactions

There is some evidence from research that simply asking children to keep track of their difficulties and talking to them about any problems that come up can reduce their problems. In one study by Dr Patrick Smith and colleagues, simply having the child track their PTSD symptoms using a questionnaire led to a reduction in them.[14] In another study by Dr Steve Berkowitz and colleagues, there seemed to be significant benefit in helping children and their carers talk openly about difficulties that the child was having.[15] It seemed that increased communication led to the child feeling more supported within their family, which in turn resulted in their difficulties decreasing. This is different to forcing the child to talk about what happened whether they want to or not. This is about gently and sensitively finding out how they are doing. It's much better for their difficulties to be out in the open rather than bottled up inside them. The next chapter describes how you can talk to your child about their difficulties.

Below is a checklist of the problems described in the previous chapter. The aim of this checklist is to:

1. Help you (and others) to pause and think about some of the difficulties that your child may be having, it may even help you to notice things that you had previously missed.

2. If you complete it on more than one occasion, it may help you to notice if things are getting better or worse over time. You could also ask another adult who knows the child well (e.g. a teacher or family member) to go through the checklist and see if you both notice the same difficulties – not as a test of each other, but simply as a way to start to discuss difficulties that either of you have noticed.

Please note, this checklist is not a formal measure of post-traumatic stress and is in no way a diagnosis. Also, you might need to be careful because you may now be paying particular attention to your child, and start to see things that you had not noticed before. This might not be because they are new or problematic but because before the events you were not particularly looking out for them. For example, your child might always have been a bit of a daydreamer who regularly gets lost in their own thoughts, but before the traumatic event you just hadn't considered it to be a problem and so didn't notice it.

It is also important to take into account the fact that some of these difficulties are more common at different ages. So always consider whether the level of the difficulty is more than would be expected for a child of their age. For instance, lots of older children start to become more moody as they approach adolescence, it is not necessarily a sign of trauma or grief.

The point of this checklist is to help you to recognise things that are noticeably different compared to before the events, or that are causing problems. If you are caring for a child and did not know them well before the events (e.g. if you are a foster carer) then obviously you may not know whether they are new or have always been there. If that is the case, you may find it useful to ask other people who knew them before and to look at other people's reports about them, such as school reports. Otherwise, you can still fill it out based on your current observations, but it might be a bit difficult to work out whether these are related to their experiences, or just the way that they are.

If you think your child would find it helpful, you could go through the checklist together.

As you approach this list, just be aware that completing a checklist like this can sometimes make people feel emotional. It's difficult to know how you will react as you work your way through. You may suddenly realise that your child has more difficulties than you previously realised. That might feel overwhelming or worrying; but once you've identified the problems, you can start to act to help them to recover.

Once you have gone through the list, ask yourself whether these things are causing a problem for the child, and whether you are worried about them.

There is a copy of this checklist in Appendix One, and further copies can be downloaded for free from https://overcoming.co.uk/715/resources-to-download.

Tick the reactions that you have noticed in your child in the last two weeks:

1) Intrusive Memories	
Having nightmares (including bad dreams which are not directly related to the event(s))	❏
Re-experiencing sensations (images, smells, sounds, tastes, touches) related to the events	❏
Flashbacks – acting or feeling as if it is happening again	❏
Having thoughts about the events that intrude into their minds or keep going round and round	❏
Repeatedly playing out or drawing particular parts of the events, or themes related to them	❏
Suddenly or repeatedly talking about the traumatic events	❏
Experiencing intense reactions to reminders	❏
2) Avoidance	
Trying not to talk about the events	❏
Trying to avoid people, activities or places that might remind them or make them think about the events	❏
Being reluctant to go to bed or sleep	❏
Keeping their minds busy with other things	❏

3) Physiological Arousal

Having difficulties in going to sleep or staying asleep ❑

Having night terrors (see description above) ❑

Sleepwalking ❑

Being irritable, losing temper easily, being angry or violent ❑

Being jumpy, or easily startled ❑

Freezing in response to perceived threats ❑

Being hypervigilant or having concentration problems ❑

Being overly sensitive to sensory stimulation ❑

4) Anxiety

Being reluctant to leave carers or clingy ❑

Having new fears ❑

Feeling panicky ❑

Losing confidence ❑

Feeling generally worried ❑

Having obsessions and compulsions; having to check that they have done certain things ❑

Suffering from headaches, tummy aches, or other physical symptoms ❑

Having a change in appetite ❑

5) Dissociation – Feeling numb and disconnected

Appearing spaced out or in a daze ☐

Forgetting things easily ☐

Not remembering what they were doing for periods of time ☐

Losing track of time ☐

Feeling detached from themselves (e.g. referring to themself as 'he' or 'she') ☐

Daydreaming ☐

Blanking out when stressed ☐

Feeling emotionally numb and disconnected (i.e. seeming flat or as if they don't have the normal range of emotions) ☐

6) Other changes in thoughts and feelings

Having inaccurate thoughts about consequences of the events ☐

Developing omen formations (i.e. thinking they knew it was going to happen) ☐

Feeling very sad, much of the time ☐

Finding it difficult to enjoy anything ☐

Feeling distant or cut-off from others ☐

Lacking motivation to do things, even things they used to enjoy ☐

Seeing everything in a very negative way ☐

Wanting to die ☐

7) Other reactions

Feeling guilty	❏
Regressing (i.e. losing some developmental skills that they had mastered)	❏
Parentification	❏
Amnesia – being unable to remember significant parts of the event	❏
Taking longer for emotions to pass	❏
Having problems at school	❏
Taking risks	❏
Deliberately hurting themselves	❏

TOTAL

Remember, this is just to help you notice and identify particular difficulties and see whether they come or go over time. Adding up the total number of yeses doesn't really mean anything concrete, although it might be interesting to note it over time. Very many children will have several of these difficulties in the immediate aftermath, but in the days, weeks and months that follow they are likely to reduce. The next parts of the book will help you to think about what you can do to make it more likely that they will reduce.

Key points

- Knowing the range of difficulties a child *could* have can help you understand what is going on for your child.

- Using the checklist in this chapter will help you identify difficulties.

- Once you have gone through the list, you can ask yourself whether these things are causing a problem for the child, and whether you are worried about them.

- You can also redo the checklist at another time to help you to notice how things are changing.

4

How to Talk to Your Child About Their Reactions

Helping your child with any difficulties or problems probably starts with you recognising that they are having difficulties in the first place and working out if they are related to their traumatic experiences. You can do this by both observing their behaviours, particularly any changes you might have noticed, and also by talking to them.

It is important, though, to go beyond the simple 'Are you OK?', which might result in a simple (and possibly avoidant) 'Yes, thanks'. Even the more open-ended 'How are you doing?' may result in the simple (and still avoidant) 'Fine, thanks'. Throughout the different parts in this book, you will notice that 'avoidance' can be very unhelpful.

Below are some tips about how to ask your child about their experiences:

- It can be helpful to choose a natural time when opportunities present themselves, rather than sitting down specifically to 'have a bit of a chat'. This can help your child to feel more relaxed. Be on the lookout for these opportunities, you might even need to create one if necessary.

- Be careful about putting your child on the spot. So, rather than sitting a child down and saying, 'Before you have your tea, I wanted to ask how you are doing since . . .', it might be preferable to make casual enquiries; for example: when you are in a car for a while and perhaps prompted by something on the radio, as in the example below.

- Use open questions. As you will see in the example below, most of the questions from the carer are open ended, which means that the child usually has to explain more, rather than simply say 'yes' or 'no'.

- Take your lead from the child. It can be a delicate balance between encouraging a conversation that the child may feel a bit uncomfortable but is OK to continue with and putting them under pressure.

- Try not to rush in with your view on things, or helpful bits of advice too soon. The task here is to listen and understand, not to speak and correct.

- Try to make sure you have enough time for the conversation and are not going to be rushed or distracted.

Example of how to talk to a child about their reactions to trauma

Carer: That news report on the radio reminds me of the fire that you had in school at the end of last term. I've been wondering, how are you doing since then?

Child: Fine.

Carer: It's just that I've noticed some changes recently.

Child: Huh?

Carer: How are you sleeping?

Child: OK.

Carer: Oh, 'cos I thought I'd heard you calling out in your sleep recently, and I was wondering if you were having any dreams?

Child: Some.

Carer: Oh, OK. How often?

Child: Quite often.

Carer: Quite often – every night, or quite often – most nights, or quite often a couple of nights each week?

Child: Quite often – most nights.

Carer: What are the dreams about?

Child: I don't really want to say?

Carer: OK, have you noticed any other changes since the fire?

Child: Some.

Carer: Like what?

Child: I don't really like going to after-school club anymore, and I don't seem to have as many friends as before.

Carer: OK, that sounds quite tough. We should talk about that, but before we do, is there anything else?

Child: Not really.

Carer: Sometimes after scary things happen, we keep thinking about the things even when we don't really want to. I know that you're having bad dreams, but are you ever thinking about it when you don't really want to during the day, when you're awake?

Child: Yep . . . and before you ask – quite often – a couple of times a week.

Carer: What do you do when that happens?

Child: I try to fill my head with other things like music or stories or what I'm going to have for my tea.

Carer: OK – does that work?

Child: For a little while, but the memories still come back later.

Carer: That sounds really tough; I think there are things that we can do together to help with those problems – if you wanted.

Unpicking your child's reactions

If a child catches a cold virus they may have a number of different symptoms such as a blocked nose, a cough, a sore throat, and a raised temperature. But it's rather easy to see those different symptoms as all being part of the same virus. Unfortunately, trauma is not quite as straightforward as that. The symptoms or difficulties can be varied and subtle, and you might not realise that they are related to traumatic events. Similarly, you might assume that some new thoughts, feelings or behaviour are related to the trauma but in fact they might be completely unrelated.

The trick to unpicking these things is to take the time to pause and think it through. First of all, it can be helpful to consider the timing:

- Were the difficulties around before the events happened?

- Have they got worse since particular events?

- Are they completely new?

- How does one problem affect another problem? For example, are they irritable because they're not getting enough sleep rather than because of their trauma? Or do they lose their temper and lash out and then feel guilty about that?

It can also help to find someone else for you to talk things through with. Therapists have regular supervision to help them stop and think things through, to try to understand what is happening. Some of my best supervision sessions have involved minimal input from the supervisor, but simply setting the time aside to talk it through and saying things out loud can be really helpful. So, you might want to find someone who is not going to offer their own opinion too quickly, and not going to try to solve the problems for you, but someone who is just going to listen and ask a few open-ended curious questions.

Key points

- Helping your child with any difficulties or problems starts with recognising that they are having difficulties in the first place.

- You can do this by both observing their behaviours, particularly any changes you might have noticed, and also by talking to them.

- You may need to use a range of different approaches to help your child open up and tell you how they are feeling.

5

Descriptions, Diagnoses and Disorders

Sometimes mental health professionals use a 'diagnosis', or more than one diagnosis, to describe a person's difficulties. Diagnoses are based on lists of criteria which are checklists of difficulties (or symptoms). If a person has a particular number and mix of difficulties, and they are causing a lot of distress, then they might be described as having a specific diagnosis or a 'disorder'.

Difficulties with diagnosis

Lots of people do not like the word 'disorder', and this may be particularly true for Post-traumatic Stress Disorder (PTSD) and Prolonged Grief Disorder (PGD). Some people wonder why they are called 'disorders' when they could be considered rational and understandable reactions to traumatic events or losses. Although many children will have some symptoms of PTSD after potentially traumatic events, for most of them the symptoms will *not* last long enough, or be severe enough, to lead to an actual diagnosis of PTSD. Similarly, many children will feel intense pain following the death of someone close to them, but for most, that pain will diminish over time. That is why, according to both the American Psychiatric Association and the World Health Organisation, Prolonged Grief Disorder (where the intense pain and longing persist for more than six months) is considered to be different from the normal process of grief.[16]

Mental health diagnoses are of course different to physical health diagnoses. For many physical health diagnoses, it is quite clear if you have an illness or not. There might be a blood test or some other test which gives a fairly definitive answer about whether you have a disease or not. With mental health, most of the symptoms that make up the different diagnoses rely on the child, or the adults around them, reporting the presence or not of certain actions, thoughts or feelings. And that reporting process may not be as accurate as a blood test or other medical test.

How severe do problems have to be before they are considered to be a diagnosis, and what specific problems make up different diagnoses? Well, the line between having a diagnosis and not is actually somewhat arbitrary – it has been decided by committees of experts who have considered lots of research. But a different group of experts on a different day might draw that line in a different place. As a result, there might not be much difference between a child that has the precise mix of symptoms to have a diagnosis, for example of PTSD, and a child that has plenty of difficulties, but not quite the particular ones for the diagnosis.

In fact, there may be some children that are extremely distressed, and really struggling, but their individual profile of difficulties does not quite fulfil criteria for any diagnosis. The strategies outlined in the next section of this book are intended to be useful for any child that has experienced loss or trauma, and not just those that have particular diagnoses.

Benefits of diagnosis

A diagnosis is just a word that describes a certain group of difficulties, it does not need to be the defining feature of any particular child, and there are ways in which a diagnosis can be useful. It can help everyone (not just professionals) to communicate about a child's individual difficulties quite efficiently without having to list all of the difficulties each time. A good therapist will still understand that the diagnosis is just a broad description of the difficulties and will take time to really get to know a child and their particular, unique problems.

Another benefit of diagnoses is in research. By defining precise types of concerns, researchers can study a set of problems – rather than having to study distress and problems in general. This can help us to understand specific responses to trauma and work out what type of treatment, intervention or support helps for different difficulties.

Sometimes having a diagnosis helps the child to access particular services or support. And knowing whether a child's difficulties are more like depression or more like PTSD can be really important to make sure that they get the right type of help and support. There is further information specifically about the diagnoses of PTSD and Complex PTSD on the website of the UK Trauma Council, details of which can be found in Appendix Three.

But remember, although diagnoses may hold particular meaning and influence within some professional systems, they are simply descriptions of difficulties.

What about you?

As their carer, you may have experienced the same loss or trauma as your child. Or you may have experienced different losses and traumas. So you may also have some of the reactions described in this part. You might feel that your own reactions complicate your child's recovery – it can certainly be pretty tough trying to help your child recover when you yourself are also recovering. This means that it's important that you take enough time and energy to look after yourself (see Part 5), but you don't have to completely hide your own reactions from your child. In fact if you did share the experience, and if you are having to cope with certain reactions, this might actually present you with some opportunities to help your child's recovery.

First of all, if you are feeling really sad because you miss someone that has died, there may be chances to show your child that it's OK to cry and be sad. If you are worried that they may worry when you are crying, you could provide them with a reassuring 'commentary'. You may also be in a really good position to share stories about the person that has died which may help your child (and you) to feel connected to the person that died. And if you and your child both went through the same traumatic experience, you may also have some opportunities to talk about your shared experience, as long as you are able to do so without your child feeling scared or unsafe, and without you becoming overwhelmed.

For example, in a family therapy session, seven-year-old Adam's mother started to cry. Adam looked over at her very concerned, then walked to her, gave her a cuddle and said, 'Don't cry mummy'. She put Adam on her lap, gave him a hug and said, 'Don't worry – I'm crying because I miss your dad so much and that makes me sad. But it's OK to be sad, and I know that in a little while I'll stop crying. And as well as being sad, I'll also be thinking about how lovely your dad was, and probably remember something lovely or funny that he did, and then I'll be sad and happy at the same time.' Adam replied, 'Do you think you'll remember the time that he tried to do pancakes for us all, and all of them were either burnt or on the floor, so we had to get pizza?' His mum said, 'Yes I might well remember that time and I'll also remember who it was that cleaned up the mess while you and your dad went to get the pizza!' As well as explaining why she was crying and giving the message that it was ok to be sad, Adam's mum also reassured him that she would stop crying soon and was able to share some pleasant joint memories of his dad.

Key points

- Diagnoses are used to describe a set of symptoms or problems.

- There are both difficulties and benefits to using a diagnosis.

- One of the benefits of a diagnosis is that it can help a child access particular types of support based on what the difficulties are that they are experiencing.

- You may be experiencing the same loss or trauma as your child.

- Knowing how much, or how little, of your own reactions to share with your child can be challenging.

- Later in the book, I talk more about how you can look after yourself. This is important for your own wellbeing, and so you feel more able to look after your child.

PART II

◇◇◇◇◇◇◇◇◇◇◇◇◇◇

Understanding How Trauma and Bereavement Work

Part 1 was all about how children react to trauma and loss. We've gone into quite a lot of detail about the reactions, and we've considered the importance of carefully noticing what's going on for them. Hopefully, you now have a good understanding of your child's particular reactions, including how much of a problem it is for them and how much distress it is causing them. In this part, we are going to look in detail at *how* trauma and loss lead to those reactions, and then go on to consider what you can do to help.

The aim of this part is to help you understand how events like loss and trauma have an impact on your child. The more you understand, the more you will be able to apply that understanding to *your particular child* and their particular experiences, which will help you to know what is most likely to help them.

After explaining how loss and trauma work, in the remaining parts of the book, I'll describe some evidence-based models and principles that can guide your actions. This will support you in providing an environment in which your child is most likely to recover from their loss or trauma, and maybe even thrive, despite their experiences.

The Cognitive Model of Trauma

The Cognitive Model is a psychological theory which helps to explain how some events can be traumatic for some children, but not others.[17] It also helps us to understand why some children struggle to adjust after somebody close to them has died: it's as if something about their experience of the death, or the sense they make of it, gets in the way of a more natural grieving process. Not only does this model help us to understand children's reactions to loss and trauma, importantly, it can also help us to understand what can be done to help.

The word 'cognitive' simply means that it is related to the way that we think about things and the way that we remember things.

There is a lot of academic research that supports this approach,[18] and therapies that are based on this model tend to be really helpful for lots of children who are struggling.[19] Therefore, we can be increasingly confident about its validity and its usefulness. This approach focuses on two particular ideas – memories and meanings. I will explain this in the next two chapters.

Tasks of Mourning

This is an approach to thinking about children's grief. It does not describe stages through which children need to pass, but it does describe certain tasks that seem to be related to healthy grieving and getting through a loss.

Dual-processing Model of Grief

This model describes how grief often does not proceed in a straight line. Bereaved children do not neatly pass through different stages, nor does their distress simply lessen over time. Instead what happens is that they spend some time being sad and really grieving their loss, perhaps struggling to see how they will manage. And then, sometimes quite suddenly, they spend time looking forwards, perhaps making plans of what they will do now. But then they return to the being preoccupied by the loss, and then they move back to looking forwards. And so on. I will describe the Tasks of Mourning and the Dual-processing Model of Grief in Chapter 8.

6

Cognitive Model of Trauma – Memory

Let's start by considering the memory part of this approach. Do you ever have the experience of a memory popping into your mind? You don't seek it out on purpose, it just seems to come from nowhere. Something in your environment may trigger it, but you may not be aware of what the trigger is. You may even recall the memory quite vividly. Lots of us have that sort of experience, but most of us don't have such experiences *most* of the time. Human beings seem to have developed a preference for keeping memories of events tucked away until we need or want them and deliberately bring them to mind. This is actually quite useful, because it would be difficult to function and get much done if our memories just intruded into our thoughts as and when they felt like it.

The ability to keep memories under control serves us pretty well in some ways, because it allows us to focus on the more important things that we are doing, and only bring the useful memories to mind when we need or want them. If there is an imminent threat, like a lorry hurtling towards us, we don't want to be distracted by memories of past events, we need to just focus on dealing with the threat at hand. Maybe we developed this ability through evolution. I was once trying to suggest this to a fourteen-year-old (luckily I have worked with some very patient fourteen-year-olds). I told her that if a group of prehistoric humans were being chased by dinosaurs, and half of them kept remembering everything as they were running away, they'd be thinking, 'Ooh – do you remember that picnic we had down there, and that game of football we had up on that hill?', they would be so flooded with memories that they may well get distracted and eaten by the pursuing dinosaurs. But if the other group of prehistoric humans could put those memories to one side and run, they would be the humans that survived, and they would go on to have children with similar sorts of skills. Humans with those skills survived and procreated, humans without them didn't survive. In this way, evolution may have led to humans generally keeping memories stored away. My client sat very patiently through my explanation of evolution, and at the end, she said: 'That's a very interesting story, but I have two problems with it. The first is that humans didn't exist at the same time as dinosaurs [which was news to me!] and the second is that I don't believe in evolution, I believe that God made us this way.' Whatever the explanation, it does seem that generally we keep memories tucked away – if anything, the problem we have with memories is that we can't find them when we need to.

And thanks to research, we know quite a lot about how memories of normal events differ from memories for traumatic events.[20]

How memories of normal events and memories of traumatic memories are different

We know that normal event memories are generally stored as words which tell stories with a meaning. We know that although they are not necessarily very accurate, the stories that we tell, which represent the memory, are usually coherent and make sense. For example, in the story above of my client, I don't remember what she looked like, I don't remember what room I was in, I don't remember her tone of voice. I don't remember the 'data' of that event, but I do remember the 'story' of the event. However, at times of overwhelming distress, horror, fear, disgust, shame, or pain, we switch into survival mode. At that point, our minds and bodies are ready to do what it takes to survive. And it seems that memories for those events, are therefore stored differently in our minds – at least to begin with. They are stored as the sensory information – the sights, sounds, smells, tastes and touches, together with the thoughts, feelings and bodily sensations. It is this 'data' of the event that is stored and makes up the memory, rather than the neat and tidy *story* of the event. And these elements of the memory may be remembered extremely vividly. Instead of being relatively complete, with a beginning, middle and an end, memories for distressing and traumatic events may consist of just a few fragments, or they may be disorganised and jumbled up.

Memories for traumatic events can also be very invasive – they may even seem as if they have a mind of their own, imposing themselves whenever they feel like it. They are very volatile and very easily triggered. The triggers may be external – in the environment (e.g. hearing a car rushing by may trigger a memory of a car crash), or the triggers may be internal (e.g. breathing heavily because of exercise may trigger a memory of hiding from someone when the child was also breathing heavily because of their anxiety).

Usually, when we remember a non-traumatic event, we know roughly where and when it happened – it was back there, and back then. It's as if memories are date-stamped when they are laid down in our brains, and even if the date-stamp gets a bit faded, we still know roughly when it happened. But traumatic memories seem to lack that sense of time, they may not have the date stamp on them and so they lack the sense of when it happened. This, together with the fact that elements of the event are re-experienced so vividly, means that it may feel as if the memory is being relived in the here and now, rather than a memory being recalled from back there and back then. How many times do you hear people describe distressing or traumatic events and say, 'I can remember it as if it were yesterday', even when it may have actually been several years before?

Memories for everyday events can change over time, to the point that sometimes we don't actually remember the event itself, but we just recall the telling of the story. And the emotions experienced at the time of the actual event tend to fade over time. But memories for distressing and potentially traumatic events tend not to change over time. They seem to be crystallised and 'locked-in' and may trigger the original distress experienced at the time of the event.

Traumatic memories don't seem to be linked to other memories in the same way that normal memories are; they often stand alone. This means that if the traumatic memory of being knocked over on a certain road keeps coming to mind, it is not linked to the memories of all the other times that that specific road was perfectly safe.

Often after difficult or stressful events, many people will talk to others such as friends and family (or pets) when they get home or to school. In this way they start to 'process' the memories of the events. By talking or thinking about the events, they start to create the story or narrative and this sort of 'wraps up' the sensory experiences and becomes the normal memory. Sometimes, this processing can take a few days or weeks, so initially the memory may intrude into their consciousness, and they may even have bad dreams or flashbacks about it. But over time, as they are able to settle and they talk it through with people, the memory gets processed and 'put away' properly.

Summary of how normal and traumatic memories are different

Common features of memories for normal events	Common features of memories for traumatic events
Consist of words and stories	Consist of vivid data of the events (sights, sounds, smells, touches, tastes, pain, feelings and thoughts)
Stories are complete and coherent	Memories are fragmented or jumbled
Stay put until deliberately recalled	Volatile (easily triggered) and intrude spontaneously
'There and then'	'Here and now'
Change over time	Locked in
Original emotions fade	Original distress keeps being triggered
Linked to other memories	Isolated from other memories
Willing to be shared with others	Avoided

Recently I was sat in a room waiting for a meeting to start. My colleague Annette walked in and I asked her how her holiday had been. She said, 'Oh – actually, I ended up in hospital and had to have an operation. There was a lot of blood, but it was OK in the end. I smashed my arm on the curb. I came off a motorbike when I was travelling around the island.' At that point another colleague arrived and also asked Annette how her holiday had been, she told the story again. This happened twice more as more colleagues arrived for the meeting. By the time the last colleague arrived, Annette's account of her holiday had changed, and she said, 'Oh, I had quite an adventure actually, I was travelling around the island on my motorbike and hit a pothole, which made me crash. My elbow hit the curb and I had to go to hospital for an operation, but it was all fine in the end.' In this way, she had the opportunity to think through her experiences and tell the story several times in the company of friends and colleagues that she knew and trusted. And as she did so, the memory seemed to change – the narrative developed and became more coherent and less fragmented, and it made more sense.

But if the event is too frightening, too distressing or too horrible to talk about or to think about, then the person does not get to talk it through or think it through and so it remains in the *raw data format*.

The boomerang effect of avoidance

The raw data of a traumatic memory may keep intruding – bringing with it the original fear, horror, or helplessness. Our response to this can be to try to avoid thinking or talking about it. This means that the memory remains unprocessed and then continues to intrude, even as we try to avoid it. People get stuck in a trap of avoidance. It's like having a song going around in your head – sometimes the more you try actively to stop thinking about it, the more it stays put. Some children describe this as being like a boomerang – the harder they throw it away, the harder it comes back and hits them.

Internal Avoidance Trap (Maintenance Cycle)

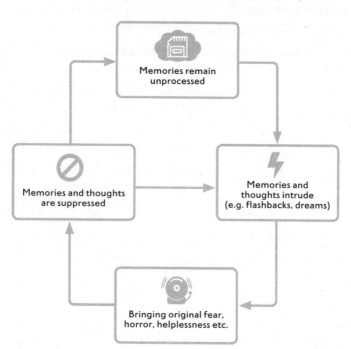

Memories remain unprocessed

Memories and thoughts are suppressed

Memories and thoughts intrude (e.g. flashbacks, dreams)

Bringing original fear, horror, helplessness etc.

We may start to avoid anything that triggers a memory of the event. A child may stop talking to certain people, they may withdraw from all sorts of activities because they are desperately trying to avoid triggering the horrible memories. For example, if the traumatic events happened at school, they may start to avoid going to school. And even the very act of trying to avoid something can trigger the memory. If a child thinks, 'I really don't want to go to school because I don't want to be reminded of. . .', they end up reminding themselves of the thing they're trying to avoid. Their strategy of avoidance doesn't work, and actually backfires.

External Avoidance Trap (Maintenance Cycle)

Avoidance to protect others

If talking about the event makes *other* people upset, then your child may also avoid talking about it, to try to protect others. Six-year-old Nina, whose stepfather had been violent to her and her mother, told me that she liked telling me about what happened. I asked her why and she said that when she told other people, her social worker said she didn't like to hear about it, her mum started to cry and her dad got really cross.

Avoidance by proxy

Often, the adults around a child end up encouraging the avoidance, even without meaning to. The adults may be worried that they will make it worse if they talk about it, they may be worried that the child will get upset, or they may be worried that they themselves will get upset, and so they deliberately avoid talking about it, or doing anything that might trigger the memory. Some adults go out of their way to 'protect' the child from distress. But this 'avoidance by proxy' may end up backfiring.

Children may start to believe that they 'shouldn't' talk about the events, and so they don't.

Explaining the nature of traumatic memories

I use a number of analogies in my work with traumatised children that help to explain the way in which traumatic memories are different to other memories, and why it might be a good idea to deliberately think them through.

The first one compares our brains to a factory making chocolate bars. The original idea for comparing the processing of memories to a factory comes from a book chapter by Professors David Richards and Karina Lovell,[21] but the extra details included below come from various families with which I have worked. The second idea is based on an analogy of a disorganised cupboard whose contents spill out and are in need of organisation. This was described by two psychologists in a very influential article by Professors Anke Ehlers and David Clark.[22] Both of these can be found in the list of references at the back of this book. But there are a number of additions in the accounts below which are from the feedback of many families and children. The third and fourth explanations come wholly from children that I have worked with.

Memories are like chocolate bars, some ingredients can't be processed without some help

A chocolate factory takes individual ingredients, like the sugar, milk and cocoa, and mixes them up to make the chocolate bars. The machine then puts a wrapper around the chocolate bars, and on the wrapper are words which tell you what's inside – it says: 'Ingredients: sugar, milk, cocoa'. This means that different chocolate bars can be sorted out and stored in the right place.

In some ways, our minds are similar – they take the sights,

sounds, smells, touches, tastes, feelings and thoughts of an experience, and process these 'ingredients' to create memories which are 'wrapped up' in the words and the stories of the event, which can then be 'stored away' until we want them.

In the chocolate factory, if the milk is too hot, or the sugar is stuck together in big lumps, the machinery can't mix the ingredients properly and it just comes to a halt. The ingredients  are left swilling around on the factory floor. The machine might try again to mix the ingredients, but if something is still too hot or too lumpy, the machine breaks down again.

In our minds, some events are just too scary, too horrible or too distressing to think or talk about, so we can't process that information into normal memories. This means that the different 'ingredients' of the experience (e.g. the sights, sounds, smells, touches, tastes, feelings and thoughts) remain unprocessed and are left floating around in our minds.

With the factory, it might be necessary to get an engineer in to help, or to wait for the milk to cool down, or to break up the sugar into smaller pieces. Then the machinery can start to mix  the ingredients and create chocolate bars again.

After potentially traumatic events, sometimes we need somebody with us to help us to think things through. Sometimes we just need to wait until they are less distressing before we can start to think them through. And sometimes, we need to break the events up into smaller pieces and go over things bit by bit rather than trying to process the whole thing in one go. Then we can create a normal memory, even of really distressing events.

Storing memories, is like storing clothes – they need folding up neatly if they are going to stay put

Imagine a well-organised wardrobe; each item is put away carefully with other similar items. When you need something, you know where to find it. You can take it out, wear it, and when you're finished you can wash it, *occasionally* iron it, and put it back in its place. There is a place for everything, and everything usually stays put. This means that you can close the doors of the wardrobe and get on with other things.

Our memories for normal events work in a similar way. Memories are stored in a particular way so that when we want to remember an event, we bring the memory to mind, and when we're finished with it, we put the memory back. The memories generally stay put until we want them, which means that we can 'close the doors' and get on with other things.

With the wardrobe, if someone throws you a duvet
full of stinging nettles and
shouts 'Put it away – quick!',
it's painful to hold, so you
might try to shove it away
quickly and close the door.

But, because it's not put away neatly, the doors don't close
properly. You might be able to hold them closed with one
hand and get on with some things, but when you take your
hand off the door, the duvet falls out, and stings you again.

Traumatic memories are like the duvet – painful to handle – and so we try to avoid them. We 'shove them away'
rather than think them through. This means that they are
not stored in the same way as other memories, so they fall
into our minds when we don't want them to. Avoiding
them may work for a while, but often just as we begin to
relax (e.g. between going to bed and going to sleep) they
intrude into consciousness again.

In order to get the duvet
to stay put and stop falling
onto you, you need to take
hold of it – which might
sting a bit – and you might
want to get someone to
help. You need to fold it

up, you might need to move some things around on the
shelves. And then you can put it away properly and it will
stay put until you want it.

In order to get traumatic memories to stay put and stop intruding, we need to find a way to deliberately bring them to mind, which might be distressing. We might want to do this with some help from someone else like a therapist or a family member. We might need to adjust our view of the world a bit, but thinking the memory through enables us to process it so that it can be stored like other memories and stay put until we choose to remember it.

Unscrunching the paper

Eleven-year-old Jamal had a history of lots of traumatic experiences before he came to the UK seeking asylum. He once explained to me how his traumatic memories were like scrunched-up pieces of paper:

He filled up the waste-paper bin with scrunched-up pieces of paper until it was over-flowing, and said, 'These are all the bad things that have happened to me, and as I walk along the road to school [he made the bin walk along and bits of paper fell out of the top] they fall in front of my eyes. And as I go to sleep [he lay the bin down and more pieces of paper fell out] they fall into my dreams. . .

. . . But when I come here and talk to you, we take each piece of paper out [he took each of the pieces of paper out], we un-scrunch them [he un-scrunched them], and we read them through carefully. . .

Then we fold them up neatly and place them back in the bottom of the bin [he folded up each piece of paper neatly and placed it in the bottom of the bin]. But because they're folded

up neatly, it means that don't fall out of the top and I have more room in my head to think about other things.

Changing the file format

Twelve-year-old Remi had witnessed a knife attack in the street. He was having very vivid, frightening nightmares. I was explaining to him that it might be helpful at some point to think through what had happened with someone, and I was using the earlier stories to explain why. Halfway through the second story, he closed his eyes, screwed his face up and put his hands over his face. I asked if he was okay, and he said, 'Yeah, yeah . . . I think I've got it. Is it like this . . . ?

. . . On my laptop at home, I've got loads of pictures saved as JPEG files. They take up loads of room on the hard drive and some of the files are corrupted, so

they keep making my computer crash.

... Are you saying that the things that happened to me are stored as JPEGs on MY hard drive [i.e. in his head]. So if I write out what happened and save them as Word documents instead ...

... they'll take up less room on MY hard drive and stop making it crash?'

I said, 'Yes – that's pretty much EXACTLY what I'm saying.'

These stories help to explain how it might be useful for your child to think through, or talk through, what has happened to them, as and when they are ready. If you think it would help them to understand what is going on, then you could share these stories with them. You could even demonstrate with messy wardrobes and duvets (although maybe don't use stinging nettles), sheets of paper and wastepaper bins, and obviously chocolate bars!

Key points

- Memories of normal events and memories of traumatic memories are different.

- Avoiding thinking or talking about memories means that the memory remains unprocessed and then continues to intrude.

- Using the analogies described in this chapter can help you explain to your child the way that traumatic memories are different to other memories, and why it might be a good idea to deliberately think them through.

7

Cognitive Model of Trauma – The importance of meaning-making

There is an important link between beliefs, thoughts, feelings and actions. Often children (and indeed adults) struggle to put their thoughts and beliefs into words, but their *actions* and *feelings* may be much more obvious. But those actions and feelings are often the result of particular thoughts and beliefs. So, it is important that we understand the beliefs and thoughts that might lie behind any feelings and actions that cause distress and difficulties.

Generally speaking, we have certain assumptions about the world. We often believe that these are truths rather than just possibilities. And we think of them as rules about how things are supposed to be. These assumptions or 'core beliefs' guide our thoughts about specific situations, our feelings and our actions. For example, I assume that the floor will hold my weight when I step on it. I don't gingerly test the ground before taking each step. This assumption is now completely unconscious, and my behaviour has become automatic. I'm not even aware that on some level I have made this assumption. These sorts of assumptions or core beliefs extend to other areas of life too; people make assumptions about other people and even about themselves. For example, they may believe that the world is safe-enough and generally makes sense; they may believe that they are an OK person and loveable enough, and that other people are reasonable and worth relating to. The beliefs may also include the way that things are *supposed* to work. For example, cars are *supposed* to stay off the pavement, carers are *supposed* to be caring and available, friends are *supposed* to be loyal.

Beliefs are influenced to a certain extent by external factors such as past experiences and what other people say (friends, family, celebrities, the media, including social media). The beliefs and assumptions act like a lens, through which children see their experiences. This lens may act to magnify some things, it might filter out some things and distort or colour other things. The way things are perceived through that lens leads to thoughts, feelings and actions.

BEFORE

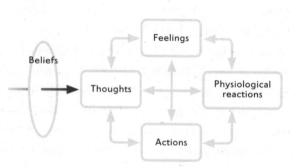

Often, the way children perceive things through this lens strengthens their beliefs and assumptions. For example, if they believe that everyone at a new school is friendly, they will start to notice the friendly acts of other children, and this confirms their beliefs because the lens has magnified that part of their experience. They might not notice children that are unkind because their lens also acts as a filter, which blocks out information that does not fit with their beliefs and is more likely to pick up information that is consistent with their beliefs. They might misinterpret other people's actions in a way that strengthens their beliefs as their lens distorts or colours their experiences. For example, if someone is actually unkind to them, they might explain it away and think that they were probably having a bad day. They might even act in a way that strengthens their beliefs; for example, if they *believe* other children are kind, they might *think* that they will be nice to them, and so will be prepared to approach and speak to other children, who then speak back to them, which further strengthens their beliefs about how friendly children are.

Impact of difficult or traumatic events

Some children may be able to make sense of events without having to change their expectations, or their lens, very much, even if the events are difficult or distressing. For example, a child who is bullied by a small group might end up still believing that most of the world is safe most of the time – just not that corridor on that afternoon. They may still believe that most people are nice enough, but those particular individuals were being egged on by their friends and so ended up lashing out. The child might even believe that generally they are safe and can look after themselves, but the group had several youths in it, so there was little that they could do to protect themselves.

For some children, however, events – or even a single event – can shatter their beliefs about the world, themselves or others, and they develop a new way of seeing things based on the traumatic events rather than on their other non-traumatic experiences. For those children, the catastrophic message of the trauma takes precedence over all other events. Then, their new lens, which is coloured by the trauma, colours the way that children see the world, themselves and other people.

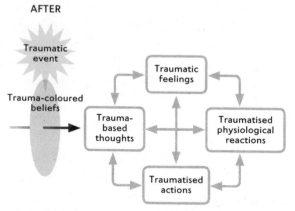

The lens may remain trauma-coloured even long after the event itself has passed. So the events still colour the way the child sees the world, which still leads to specific thoughts, feelings and actions, but it might not be easy to see that as a result of the event because it happened so long before.

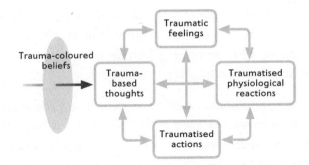

The beliefs, which tend to be about the world, themselves and others in general, lead to specific thoughts in specific situations. For example, if the meaning given by a child to a physical assault is that they are vulnerable, the world is dangerous, and people are evil, then when their friends invite them out, they may well think that if they leave the house they will be assaulted again. This makes them feel afraid, leads to raised heart rate and sweating, and in order to reduce their fear they stay in and avoid leaving their house and their carer.

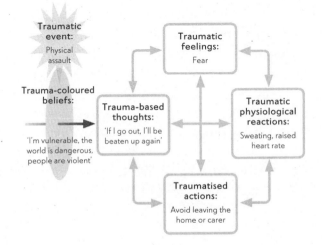

However, it might not be obvious how children think about things. Their feelings and their actions might be better indicators that something has changed in how they see things.

For example, based on previous experiences, a young child may believe that birds are little brown or grey things that usually fly away when you go towards them. They might not even realise that this is their belief, and even if they did, they would be unable to express that in words. But if that young child then has an experience where a large brightly coloured parrot flies towards them and the feathers from its wing brushes over their head, they may well be terrified at that moment, and they may start to believe that all birds have the potential to be threats. They will not be able to express that belief, but the carers may notice that next time the child sees any bird (including the small grey ones that fly away when approached) they feel terrified, they have a physiological reaction such as raised heart rate and butterflies in their stomach, so they run from the bird crying and into the arms of their carer. That avoidance of birds then serves to reinforce the belief that birds are dangerous, because running away from the bird and towards the carer led them to feel safe. This might not really be a 'traumatic' event as such, but it could lead to an important change in the child's view of things (especially birds), and this change may have lasting consequences.

This is represented in the diagram below. The incident with the parrot changes the way that the child sees their world and birds in particular. It is as if the incident colours the lens through which they see the world. And this then leads to specific thoughts, feelings and actions.

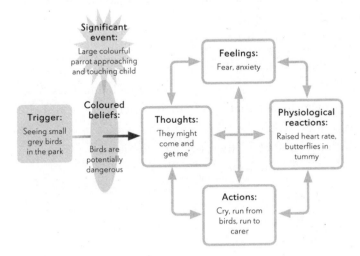

How serious an event was and how close the child was to it are important – but not the whole story

How close a person was to an event, the severity of it, and how involved they were with it, will of course make a difference to how it affects them – but only to a certain extent.

Generally speaking, actually being in a car crash is worse than being in a car next to one that crashed. And that would usually be worse than being down the road and seeing a crash, which in turn would tend to be worse than reading about the crash in your neighbourhood. And that would typically be worse than learning about a crash in a different town. But this nearness or proximity only <u>partly</u> predicts the impact.

Similarly, breaking lots of bones and suffering some internal damage would generally be more traumatic than breaking an arm in two places, which would usually be more traumatic than a broken nose, which would typically be more traumatic than a black eye. But it is quite possible for someone who is actually quite badly hurt to be able to understand that it was a random event, that they were just unlucky, and maybe even that they were lucky in some ways because it could have been worse and that their world remains a relatively safe place. Whereas it would be possible for someone who learns about an assault in another town to have intrusive images of what that would be like if it had been them, and to start to see their own world as dangerous, and themselves as vulnerable. In other words, the severity of the event and proximity to the event do of course play a role, but how a child *interprets* an event plays a more important role in predicting how much an event will affect them.

Impact of accidental or deliberate events

Research consistently shows that events in which one person has actually done something to someone else on purpose are more likely to be traumatic for people than events that are accidents or acts of nature. For example, research has shown that generally children were nearly three times more likely to develop PTSD if the traumatic event had been 'interpersonal'.[23] It seems that it's just more difficult to make sense of an event if someone else, a fellow human being, is responsible for it, or even if someone else simply appears to be responsible. So if an event is actually a complete accident, but your child thinks that someone did it on purpose, or someone is responsible for not protecting them, then they are more likely to find it traumatic. It might simply be that it is difficult to understand why someone else would do such a thing.

Of course, if the person responsible is a carer, or someone the child has a trusting relationship with like a teacher, a family member, or family friend, then the impact can be even greater. Such events can lead to a sense of betrayal and colour the way that the child sees other people, the world and themselves. They may start to think that if someone who should have been looking after them can hurt them, then surely there is nobody that can be trusted. Or they may start to believe that there is nowhere in the world that is safe. Some children start to think that there must be something wrong with them if a person that *should* have been looking out for them did something bad to them.

The knock-on effect of traumatic events

If the events shatter a child's previously held belief that generally things in the world make sense and happen for a reason, the child might start to believe that *nothing* makes sense any more and everything is unpredictable. Likewise, if the event or events seem deliberate and the child feels betrayed, they may find it hard to trust anyone. Obviously, this could be very confusing and frightening.

Such changes in beliefs and expectations can help to explain how an event can lead to difficulties that may not appear to be linked to the event. For example, a child who is assaulted in the street and receives minor injuries might stop wanting to go swimming in the pool a short walk from their home. On the face of it, the assault may seem unrelated to going swimming, but there are a number of ways that the assault could have changed their beliefs about the world, other people and themselves. They might now believe that the world is unsafe and that adults cannot be trusted to help, so when it is time to go swimming they think, 'What happens if I start to have difficulty in the middle of the pool, how can I be sure someone will notice and will come and help me?' Or they may think that they are vulnerable and that although they only had minor injuries when they were assaulted, they might not be so lucky if they go swimming. They may think that the minor injuries they received now mean that they are unable to do things like swimming and that they probably shouldn't risk it just in case they can't manage.

Nine-year-old Sara's uncle was knocked over by a car. Afterwards she did not just find that road frightening, in fact it wasn't just roads and traffic that she struggled with. She started to find everything difficult. She needed constant reassurance about what was going to happen during the day, who was going to take her to school, who would collect her from after-school club and at exactly what time. It was as if the single event of the accident made her question whether *anything* was predictable and safe.

Actions and beliefs

Below is a list of some examples of feelings and actions that may occur after traumatic events, and the possible beliefs which lie behind them.

Observable feelings and actions	Beliefs that might be behind those feelings and actions
Clingy, reluctant to leave carer	*Nowhere is safe*
Reluctant to try anything new	*I'm no good* *I usually fail at things*
Withdrawing from social contact	*Nobody cares about me* *I can't trust anyone*
Angry outbursts	*Life is not fair* *Other people are dangerous unless I keep them away from me*
Sadness and lack of motivation	*Bad things always happen to me* *I deserve bad things to happen to me*
Avoiding anything challenging	*I can't cope*
Avoiding all possible triggers	*The memory is unbearable*

Sometimes children develop inaccurate thoughts about the events and what caused them. These might be based on their imagination, or on inaccurate accounts that circulate around social media or around the playground. For example, they might believe that a fire was the result of a bomb, when in fact it was due to an electrical fault. This misunderstanding may have far-reaching consequences for their beliefs about the world in general, e.g. they may start to believe that they are not safe anywhere.

The vicious cycles of negative thoughts, feelings and actions

Worry and sadness

The link between thoughts and feelings goes both ways – negative thoughts tend to lead to negative feelings, and negative feelings tend to lead to negative thoughts. Sometimes children get caught in a bit of a vicious cycle where their thoughts lead to certain feelings, and those feelings influence their thoughts, and those thoughts keep the feeling going. For example, a child who thinks that they are unsafe might feel very anxious, and that anxiety then causes them to have more thoughts about all of the bad things that could happen to them, and those thoughts then increase their anxiety. Then, their thoughts about not being safe cause them to not leave the house, and then staying in and being safe confirms their belief that they are safe indoors, but not outdoors, etc. Or a child who thinks that nobody likes them may feel very sad and they start to think more about the people that don't like them and what that means, which makes them feel more sad. And because they are feeling sad, they don't want to spend time with friends, which makes them feel more sad and believe that they don't really have good friends.

There are all sorts of different ways that thoughts, feelings and actions can feed into each other. Are you able to map out some of these cycles for your child?

Guilt

Sometimes, guilt is the natural result of desperately trying to make sense of the world and clinging to a belief that things make sense. The notion that the world can be unpredictable and events are random may be terrifying, so as a way to retain a belief that the work makes sense and that things happen for a reason, children may construct an account of events which includes the idea that it was their own fault. As far as the child is concerned, if it was their fault then at least that means that the event was not random, it happened for a reason and the world continues to make some sort of sense. But the resulting guilt they feel makes it really difficult to bring the event to mind and think it through because they feel so bad about it. This avoidance then prevents them from reappraising the responsibility for the event more realistically. Each time a thought about the event comes to mind, they are so upset that it was their fault, that they push the thoughts away, rather than thinking things through more accurately. Sometimes people around the child, in an attempt to help them to develop more realistic and more helpful thinking, actually end up supporting the child's strategy of not thinking it through by simply telling them to stop thinking like that. Simply insisting that it was not their fault in a rather blunt way might actually make them think that they will not be taken seriously and so they stop talking about their thoughts that it was their fault.

Eight-year-old Seb's mother thought that Seb had gone into the house when she was parking the car; but he was picking something up from the floor. His mother accidently ran him over. The first time I met Seb on his own, he said 'It's my fault; I walked around the back of the car and picked up a stone. If I had walked round the front of the car, or if I hadn't picked up the stone, then Mum would have seen me and would not have run me over.' I asked him if he had ever told anyone else that that was what he thought. He said, 'I used to, but everyone told me that I was stupid for thinking that and that I should stop it.' I asked if he did actually stop thinking that, and he said, 'No – I just stopped telling people that's what I was thinking.'

Avoidance

I discussed earlier how avoidance can keep alive the traumatic memories, but avoidance can also maintain the traumatic meaning. Many children might be scared initially following a frightening event. For example, if a stranger comes into the school playground shouting and acting aggressively and is forcefully removed by the police, then it is quite possible that some children will suddenly start believing that the school is not a safe place. But through talking about the event with teachers, friends and families, in addition to changing the quality of the memory, they are then able to understand that this was a one-off event. So when they first return to school, although they may be a little anxious, they overcome that and realise that the school is as safe as it has always been. However, some may believe that the school is unsafe and so the next day they refuse to go to school. The carer may be sympathetic and allow the child to stay at home for a day, expecting them to return the day after. But by avoiding going back to the school the child holds on to their belief that the school is unsafe, and so may refuse to go to school on subsequent days. This avoidance just serves to re-enforce their belief that the school is unsafe. Ten-year-old Jo, who had been shouted at violently by a stranger on the bus, said to me, 'The only reason it's not happened again is that I've not left the house'. He started to believe that the reason the person had shouted at him was because there was something wrong with Jo, and he imagined that other people could see that too and didn't like him. So when opportunities to go out came along, for example to play with friends or go to family events, he thought that others did not really want him there. That made him sad and despondent. So he stopped going out. But then after a while, people didn't bother inviting him out because he hardly ever went. This made him even more isolated and confirmed his ideas about being unpopular.

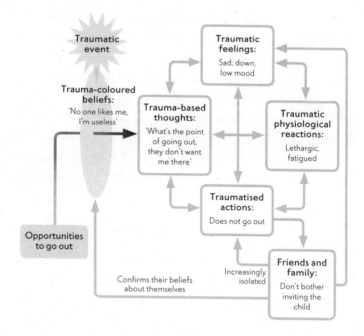

Traumatic event

Trauma-coloured beliefs:
'No one likes me, I'm useless'

Trauma-based thoughts:
'What's the point of going out, they don't want me there'

Traumatic feelings:
Sad, down, low mood

Traumatic physiological reactions:
Lethargic, fatigued

Traumatised actions:
Does not go out

Opportunities to go out

Friends and family:
Don't bother inviting the child

Increasingly isolated

Confirms their beliefs about themselves

Key points

- Generally speaking, we have certain assumptions about the world and we often believe that these are truths rather than just expectations or possibilities.

- These assumptions or 'core beliefs' guide our thoughts about specific situations, our feelings and our actions.

- A child's experience of trauma or loss may affect their core beliefs and how they make sense of their world.

- Understanding how thoughts, feelings, actions and physiological reactions maintain problems is important in supporting recovery.

8

Models to Help Understand and Live with Loss

With very few exceptions, everyone will experience bereavement at some point in their lives. A huge survey analysed by the National Children's Bureau in the UK showed that by the time they reach sixteen years old, on average one child in every class will have experienced the death of a parent or sibling, and two children in every class will have experienced the death of a friend.[24]

Different children's reactions to a bereavement can be very different. Reviewing lots of the research available at the time, Dr Linda Dowdney in 2000 concluded that bereaved children tended to suffer from a broad range of psychological difficulties rather than developing one specific problem or disorder.[25] Of course, bereaved children tend to be more sad than those that are not bereaved, and some may develop depression, but they are also more likely to develop other difficulties such as anxiety (particularly in relation to the way that the person died), guilt, concentration problems and sleep difficulties. For many bereaved children, these difficulties tend to diminish over the months following the death, but about 20 per cent of bereaved children may still be struggling quite significantly a year, or even two years after the death. The research has struggled to work out what long term impact childhood bereavement has because there are so many factors that complicate the picture. However, the research does consistently show that how well a bereaved child does is closely linked to how well their carer is doing. This is a really important point – it means that whoever is looking after a child who has been bereaved really does need to look after themselves, so that they can do the best for the child. I'm going to talk about this quite a lot in the last part of the book.

Some researchers have tried to describe different stages that children pass through after they are bereaved. These might be denial, anger, sadness, resolution. This can be helpful because it helps children and those around them to realise how normal it is to experience a range of strong emotions after a bereavement, and not just sadness. But we need to be careful because very often bereaved children do not progress neatly through each stage. Some may work through every stage, but in a different order, others will return to stages that they have already been through, and others will miss out some stages altogether.

Tasks of mourning

Professor William Worden, following a lot of work and research with bereaved children, described four 'tasks of mourning' rather than discrete stages of reaction.[26] This provides a useful description of the 'work' that is necessary when adjusting to the loss of someone important and it explains some of the reactions as well as what helps.

William Worden's Tasks of Mourning:

- Accept the reality of the loss

- Process the pain of grief

- Adjust to a world without the person that died

- Find a lasting connection with the person that died while continuing with life

---

Accept the reality of the loss

Sometimes it can take quite a bit of time and even effort to accept the fact that someone has actually died. Some children will find it such a shock that they simply cannot believe that the person has died. Others may want to pretend that it has not really happened. Or they may accept that reality at one moment but then seem to forget that the person has died. They have just got so used to the person being part of their life, it can take them a while to get used to the idea that they have died. Children may seem to jump in and out of realisation: one minute apparently understanding that the person has died, and the next minute asking when they are coming home. Sometimes that can be because they do not have a full understanding of death and what it means, but other times it's because the realisation that the person has died is not a smooth gradual process, and it comes and goes before finally settling down.

Accepting the reality of the loss may be especially difficult if the death is not a 'natural' one (e.g. killed by someone or in an accident). But it may also be difficult to accept if the child had not really realised that everyone dies, and in particular had not contemplated the fact that someone they know will die. A child's previous experiences of death will influence how they are able to accept the reality of the death. For example, a child that has had several pets that have died, will realise much more quickly what it means when someone dies.

Process the pain of grief

Different people grieve in different ways – some get very angry, some get very sad, some get very anxious, and some do bits of all of those and more besides. The grief may come out in all sorts of unexpected ways. And it may last longer than expected too. Research indicates that about one in five bereaved children are still struggling significantly in one way or another a year after the death. It can be difficult if those around the child expect them to have 'got over it' within a few weeks or months, because those people are then more likely to misinterpret the child's feelings and behaviours. The child may also feel that they *should* have got over it and may then feel that there is something wrong with them, or that they cannot be open about their feelings and have to keep them to themselves.

The pain experienced when someone close to you dies can be very intense. Many children may try to avoid it and suppress it rather than actually go through it. The difficult emotions may come and go, it's as if children are dipping into it for a bit, and then dipping out when it becomes too much for them, only to return to it later.

Adjust to a world without the person that died

After the death of a loved one, the child's world may be significantly changed, and this can take time to get used to. There may be some obviously significant external things that have changed, such as who will put them to bed, where they live, whom they live with and which school they go to. There may also be more subtle changes such as who will meet them from school on a Friday, where they visit at half-term, or how emotionally available their carer is (who may be preoccupied with their own grief). Children may also have to get used to some changes to their 'internal' world, or their sense of 'self'. They may be used to being 'Sam's little brother' or 'Alex's daughter', and they need to work out if that is still true if it is Sam or Alex who has died. They may need to adjust their assumptions about the world and people in it: they need to get used to the fact that other people in their life will die, and that ultimately, they will too. Many people operate very well in blissful ignorance (or deliberate avoidance) of these facts but when someone close to you dies it becomes difficult to ignore the facts. Getting used to them means accepting them, and then being able to get on with things, rather than becoming preoccupied with them in an unhelpful and distressing way.

Find a lasting connection with the person that died while getting on with life

Over time, many children continue to feel a connection to the person that died. The relationship that they had has changed but does not have to end. Some will continue to talk to them or imagine what they would think or say about things. This continuing bond seems to help many people who are bereaved to carry on with life, they move forwards (as opposed to 'move on' or even 'get over') while sometimes looking back. Memories of the person and of shared activities become very important. For some children, objects that are related to the person that died can take on a great deal of significance.

Dual-processing Model of Grief

A useful way of thinking about grief is called the Dual-processing Model.[27] This theory, first described academically by Professors Margaret Stroebe and Henk Schut, suggests that instead of simply working through stages, phases or tasks of grief in turn, in reality what happens is people go to and fro between two different types of coping. One type of coping is all about dealing with the losses associated with the bereavement – the loss of a relationship, the loss of support, the loss of company. It might involve spending time thinking repeatedly about the person that has died and how they died. It might involve longing for them, poring over photographs of them and being really sad that they have gone or very angry about the way that they died. Although painful (to experience and to watch) this is often part of the grieving process. The bereaved child starts to accept and understand their loss, they may also experience pleasurable emotions such as joy when remembering times spent together. The other type of coping is all about coming to terms with the new world – one where the person is no longer physically present. This might also involve making sense of the fact that the world is one in which bad things can happen and people die – not really a 'new' world, but just the old world seen through 'new' eyes. This coping involves looking forwards rather than backwards, and perhaps making plans that do not involve the person that died. It involves getting used to the changes that are the result of the bereavement – actual material changes but also changes in the way that the child sees themselves, others and the world.

As children grieve, they may alternate between these two types of coping. One minute they may be looking at photographs of them playing football with their father who died and being very sad, the next minute they may be off playing football with friends. One of the very useful things about the dual-processing theory is that it prepares us for the fact that children who are bereaved can step back into their grief and processing of the loss, having stepped out of it and apparently got on with coping with the changes to their life. The theory can therefore help us to be reassuring when this happens. If a bereaved child has been busy getting on with their new life and then suddenly finds themselves reminiscing and being really sad again, this is not a step 'backwards' – quite the opposite. I have found families have been hugely reassured by knowing that this swing between the two modes is normal; many have appreciated knowing it in advance and knowing what to expect.

Traumatic Bereavement

Not all deaths are traumatic, some are just very sad. But if there is something about the way in which the person died which is traumatic, then this can make it more difficult for children to grieve their loss. Sudden deaths, violent deaths, accidental deaths, deaths by suicide and deaths caused by someone else all have the potential to be traumatic. But even deaths that seem 'natural' to others may be experienced by children as traumatic. It depends on the child's experience of the death and what meaning they make of it.

Farah was six years old when her Granny died peacefully in her sleep at the age of eighty-six, having previously been in excellent health and spent her last day with her grandchildren. For many of the adults this was seen as a 'good death'. The meaning that they made of the death was very positive – 'she had a good innings', 'I'm so glad that she didn't suffer – she would have hated that', 'how lovely that her last day was spent playing with her grandchildren whom she loved so much'.

But, for Farah, there was no such positive meaning to the death. She was not only heartbroken by the loss of her beloved Granny, but she also suddenly realised that people die, that all people die, that her parents will die, and that she herself will die. She realised that death was not only inevitable, but it was also unpredictable (Granny had not been ill). She then found it impossible to leave her mother's side for fear that one of them would die. She slept in her parents' bed, she accompanied her mother to the toilet and of course refused to go to school. The parents understandably assumed that this would just be a phase and so just went along with it. But several weeks later, when it was clear that it was not just a phase, they sought some professional help. Farah responded well to some open and honest conversations with her parents who answered her questions. They talked more openly about exactly what had caused Granny's death, they reluctantly admitted when questioned that yes, they would die one day, but they did not expect it to be any time soon – and they explained why they did not expect that to be soon, so that Farah could understand their meaning-making and was more convinced by it. They moved on to discuss all the things that she was missing out on by not leaving her mother's side and they worked on a plan of how to help her to 'reclaim' her life.

For some bereavements, there may be images associated with the death itself that become traumatic images as described in Chapter 6. Then, whenever children try to think about the person that died, rather than being sad about their loss, they find themselves scared or frightened by the death itself.

And if the death shatters a child's assumptions in an unhelpful way, about how things are supposed to be, then this meaning can be traumatic, as described earlier. For example, if the death was sudden and unexpected, then the message of the event of the death may be *the world is unpredictable*. Or if the person was killed by someone known to them, the message may be *you can't trust anyone*. If these messages then colour the way the child sees everything, rather than just the single event, it can lead to lasting and more complicated difficulties.

Ali's family were especially badly hit by COVID-19. Several of his relatives caught the disease and his grandfather died during the height of the pandemic when health services were extremely stretched. These events coloured his beliefs – he started to see the whole world as unbearably dangerous. He thought of himself as particularly vulnerable, even though the disease seemed to have less impact on the health of children. And he believed that doctors could not be trusted to keep him and his family safe. When the schools reopened and he was expected to return to school, because of his beliefs that were based on the traumatic events, his immediate automatic thoughts were that he would get the virus and die, or pass it on to other family members who would die. This obviously made him feel terrified. So, he understandably refused to return to school and deliberately avoided his friends so that he could reduce the risk. He had vivid intrusive memories of the night that the ambulance came and took his grandfather to hospital, as well as nightmares about what it must have been like for his grandfather to die at the hospital on his own. Not going to school did reduce Ali's anxiety. But it strengthened his belief about what would happen if he did go to school, and so his avoidance maintained his beliefs about school and his own vulnerability. This is shown figuratively below.

Pandemic-related Death

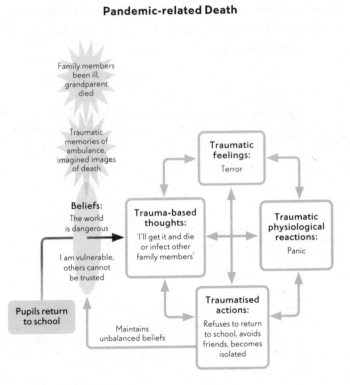

If your child has been traumatically bereaved, then the sections of this book specifically about trauma may be just as relevant as the sections about bereavement. It may be necessary for traumatically bereaved children to process the event of the death *before* they are able to start to grieve their loss.

Key points

- Everyone will experience bereavement at some point.

- Different children can react to a bereavement in very different ways.

- Models of grief, such as the Tasks of Mourning and the Dual-processing Model can help you understand what your child might be experiencing.

9

Making Sense of Your Child's Difficulties – Formulations

Hopefully you've now been able to notice your child's reactions, perhaps by completing the checklist in Chapter 3. You may also have been able to talk to your child about how they are doing, as described in Chapter 4. The next step is to try to map out what is going on.

Many mental health professionals try to draw up a *formulation* of children's difficulties. A formulation is really just a story that explains what is going on, and why. A good formulation will also lead to ideas of what might help. But you don't have to be a professional to do this. In fact, most people do it automatically – they just don't call it a formulation. Anyone who has stopped to think about why a child is doing something, and then tried to help, has done a formulation. The best formulations though are not usually just drawn out of thin air, they are based on psychological theories. A formulation should open up your thinking and ideas, and not be treated as some sort of absolute truth that has to be stuck to.

So now that you understand some of the psychological theories that explain how trauma and loss 'work' (or how trauma and loss can lead to difficulties), before working out what to do, let's try to use the models to understand what is going on for your child. This will boost your possibilities of helping them.

Sometimes, it can be useful to map things out using a diagram. As you will have seen in examples throughout the book to this point, I have used a standard structure for the formulations that is based on the approach described. And here is a blank version for you. Can you use it to map out some of your child's trauma-based or bereavement-based beliefs, thoughts, feelings and actions? You might want to add how the memories contribute to the problems if that is relevant. The younger your child is, the more difficult it can be to work out what their beliefs and thoughts are, so as their carer you might need to make a few well-informed guesses which you can check out over time. Don't get too hung up on getting it exactly right, and don't worry if you can't fill in all of the boxes. This is just a way to try to help you pause, reflect and try to make sense of how the events have affected your child. The understanding that comes with the formulation may help you and those around your child to respond to their needs, rather than react.

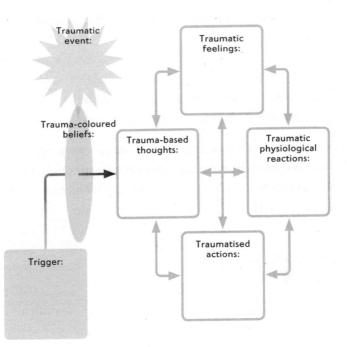

Before, during and after

As well as making a note of your child's difficulties (detailed in Part 1), it can sometimes be helpful to make a note of what happens immediately before and afterwards, to help you to realise what the triggers and the consequences are. This sort of systematic record is sometimes rather grandly called a 'functional analysis' and is something that you might be able to do together with your child. It might be useful to write this down in a simple chart to help you begin to make sense of it. I know it seems really basic, but taking the time to make a note of things helps you to stop and think things through in a more methodical way. You just need four columns:

- **Where and when**

- **Before:** What was happening before? What was the child doing? Did anything in particular trigger them?

- **During:** What exactly did they do? Describe the *behaviour*, not what you assume they were feeling or thinking

- **After:** Who did what afterwards? Was there any gain for your child (e.g. did they end up in your bed, did they avoid having to go somewhere)?

There is a blank table in the Appendix One at the end of the book in case that's easiest, and further copies can be downloaded from https://overcoming.co.uk/715/resources-to-download. But you can easily make one yourself.

You can then use the information given in the previous chapters and your formulation to see if that helps to explain possible links between events and problems.

- Could the volatile and vivid nature of *memories* for traumatic events explain some of the difficulties?

- What do the events *mean* for your child? Some of this might be guesswork because your child might not be able to tell you about the meaning of certain events. But you might be able to 'join the dots' and understand how specific events have changed the child's view of themselves, others or their world, and those changes lead to changes in their feelings and their actions or behaviours.

- Do any of the difficulties serve a purpose, such as avoiding triggering memories, or facing things that they now think are dangerous?

Here is an example:

Where and when	Before	During	After
	What was happening before? What was the child doing? What were others doing? Did anything seem to trigger them?	What exactly did they do? (Describe behaviour, not thoughts and feelings.)	Who did what afterwards? Was there any possible gain for the child?
Playground Sat, 3pm	Playing on swing with best friend, who shoved him	He shouted, punched, ran off	He was unapproachable so I left him to calm down
Bedroom Sun, 10pm	Lying in bed, had just read him a story and left his room	Kept shouting and crying	I went back in and stayed until he fell asleep

Key points

- A formulation is really just a story that explains what is going on, and why.

- The models described in this book are a good foundation on which you can base a formulation.

- A good formulation will also lead to ideas of what might help.

- Taking the time to stop and think it through can help you and those around your child to respond to them rather than react.

- A formulation should open up your thinking and ideas, and not be treated as some sort of absolute truth that has to be stuck to.

- Mapping out what routinely happens before, during and after your child's reactions can help you identify particular triggers and patterns.

PART III

◇◇◇◇◇◇◇◇◇◇◇◇

What You Can Do to Help

It's possible that you might have skipped straight to this section and not read the previous chapters that are the foundations for what follows. That is completely under-standable – you want to help your child and you just want to know what to do. I understand that. But if you are able to find the time to read the earlier chapters of this book, then it will really help you to understand what is behind your child's problems and what approach is going to work best for them. And the more you understand that, the more you can adapt the ideas in this book to fit with what *your* child needs. One size really does not fit all when it comes to working out what will help, but the approaches described in the previous part do seem to help our understanding of most children who have experienced trauma or loss.

In Part 1, I explained four different paths that describe how reactions to loss and traumatic events progress over time. Of course, it's not quite as simple as that, but it can be use-ful to think about your child's reactions in that way. The four different paths were: Lasting, Delayed, Recovery and Unaffected. I pointed out that research shows that many children who start off with lots of difficulties will recover over time – they are on the Recovery path. The rest of this book is all about how you can increase their opportunities for recovery and reduce the chances of any difficulties enduring. Do you have a sense yet of which path your child might be on?

10

Maximising Chances of Recovery

What can you do to help?

However much you wish you could, you can't change what has already happened to your child. But you CAN do a great deal about what happens now. Below I describe how you can create an environment around your child that will maximise their chances of healing and recovery. However, it's also important to realise that this does not mean you are solely responsible for whether or not they recover, and one of the ways you might need to help your child is by asking for help for them – or for you.

Hopefully, having completed a formulation of the difficulties your child is experiencing, you have a better sense of what is behind them. Now, we are going to focus on things you can do to help.

The ripples might cause more problems than the dropped rock!

If you drop a rock in a pond, after the initial splash there are lots of ripples that spread out across the pond; those ripples bounce off the sides and come back, and they may collide with some of the ripples still coming from the original splash. Similarly, after some losses and traumatic events, there are lots of additional stressors that follow; for example, a child might have to move house, they might have to move school, there could be a lot of interest from the media, there might be a police investigation and eventually a criminal prosecution. Sometimes it is these ripples or 'after-shocks' that cause the child more difficulties than the identified traumatic events themselves. For example, a child might have been involved in a car crash that was very frightening and very painful, and they might make a good psychological and physical recovery. But, then they might become famous within their school as the kid that was nearly killed, which might attract lots of unwanted attention so they might start to avoid school, and then start to struggle academically because they have missed lessons, and then they might get lower grades in their exams which means they cannot get on the college course they wanted, which ultimately affects their career choices. The ripples might cause more problems than the rock.

So, it is worth doing what you can within reason to minimise subsequent stressors on your child and try to keep things as stable as possible. When changes and subsequent stresses cannot be easily or practically avoided, it's important to approach them with a bit more care and attention, taking time to explain to your child what is going to happen and why. It is also important to be curious with them about the impact of these after-effects, and not just assume that the only event to worry about is the identified trauma.

The Five Principles Approach for creating an environment that supports recovery

A huge body of research evidence was reviewed in 2007 by Professor Stevan Hobfoll, together with nineteen colleagues from around the world.[28] They recommended five principles that can be used to shape the sort of environment and support that will promote recovery and give your child the best chance of adjusting to what has happened. As well as guiding your general approach, the principles can also be used in specific situations to help you make particular decisions. For example, if you and your child have had to move home suddenly you may be trying to work out whether it would be better to keep your child at their old school, enrol them in a new school or home-school them for a while. You could consider each of these principles to help you consider the pros and cons of each choice.

At times, you too might be distressed about what has happened to your child, and it may have affected you directly too. This, together with a strong desire to make it OK for your child, might be quite overwhelming at times. It might be difficult to work out what would be best for your child. If you have managed to complete a formulation and the 'Before – During – After' table as described in Part 2, that can help to you have a more objective and reasoned understanding of your children's difficulties. And even when you are struggling or feeling overwhelmed, you can use these principles to guide your decisions.

The Five Principles focus on helping your child to feel:

1. Safe

2. Calm

3. Socially supported and connected

4. In control

5. Hopeful

You may be surprised at just how simple these ideas are. But when something 'extraordinary' has happened to children, they don't need *more* extraordinary things from the adults around them, what they need is extra 'ordinary' things. Each one of these will be explained in more detail in the following chapters.

Key points

- Try mapping out the formulation or story that explains what is going on with your child and why.

- A good formulation will lead to ideas of what might help.

- The Five Principles is a comprehensive, evidence-based approach to offering help.

- It is not prescriptive and does not tell you exactly what to do, or when.

- But it does provide a framework to guide what you do to support your child.

- It suggests that you help your child to feel:

    1. Safe

    2. Calm

    3. Socially supported and connected

    4. In control

    5. Hopeful

Feeling Safe

First, make sure that your child *is* actually safe, and protected as much as reasonably possible from further events. But this principle is not just about their *actual* safety, it's also about their *felt sense of safety*.

Basic needs and basic routines

Make sure that their basic needs are being met before you worry about anything else. Do they have food, drink and shelter – and do they know that? It's difficult to help a child feel safe if they are not sure where their next meal is coming from, or if they don't know where they will be sleeping or who is going to be around when they go to bed.

Cuddly toys, or other personal possessions can be extremely important to children, and they may take a great deal of comfort from being reunited with them. That might be complicated, for example if their home has become a crime scene and has been cordoned off by the police. However even then it might be possible to retrieve one or two special items by explaining the situation to the police. Or if necessary, get them a new cuddly toy specifically to help them through.

Children feel safer when routines are in place, when things are familiar and when they know what is happening next. So as much as is possible, reinstate routines and structure to their day. It may not be possible to return to old routines, so you might need to establish new ones. Keeping things as consistent as possible will reduce the amount of uncertainty that your child has to cope with. For example, if they *know* that dad takes them to school, and mum picks them up from school, then they don't have to expend any energy wondering about this and their world can start to feel a bit more predictable and stable. Of course, it's likely to be impossible to stick to such routines every single day, but the more consistent and predictable things are, the more they will be able to cope with the exceptions.

After loss or trauma, it might feel to the child as if their whole world has fallen apart and nothing is predictable anymore. They might, therefore, be much more sensitive to even small, unexpected changes, let alone the bigger changes or disruptions that they may have to go through such as changing home or school. You can help them to feel as safe as possible by:

- Explaining what is going to happen, asking them if they have any questions or concerns, and then answering any questions honestly and appropriately.

- Explaining *why* the change is happening may help them to hold on to a belief that some things are consistent and predictable.

- It can be helpful to create a calendar with them so that they know what is happening in the coming days. This is particularly useful if their usual routine has had to be abandoned. You can get them to help draw the pictures depicting different activities and they can cross off each day so that they get a sense of when different things will happen.

Meaning-making as a way to feel safer

So, you have to help them to *feel* safe. In Chapter 7, I explained how their experiences might have coloured their view of themselves, the world or other people. So even if in reality they <u>are</u> safe, they might <u>see</u> things differently. They may see reality through a very differently coloured lens and consequently might evaluate the risk differently. If you have managed to complete a formulation and the Before-During-After table from Chapter 9, then this will really help you to understand what is going on; and it might help you to recognise how the traumatic events or the loss have coloured their view of things.

Seven-year-old Sabina had been abused by both of her parents for a couple of years before she went to live with some amazing foster carers who were kind, sweet and loving. After two years in the foster placement, she still had not really settled and seemed as distressed as ever. One of the professionals involved asked why the two years of amazing care had not balanced out the two years of abuse. After working with her for several weeks, it became clear to me that she saw the lovely care from the foster carers through her particular traumatised lens. She interpreted their loving actions as being malicious. She said to me, 'My foster carers are only doing it for the money, and they're trying to get me to like them so that they can hurt me – that's what people do'. And because this was her interpretation of their actions, she understandably worked hard to keep them at arm's length, not wanting to allow them to get close to her. Her strategy of trying to keep her carers at a distance made complete sense when she was living with her parents, but now that she was in a safe place, this strategy was no longer helping her. She could not see that, because her view of her foster carers had been coloured by her abuse by her parents. It changed the way she saw all carers, not just those that had abused her.

'What' comes before the 'how' and the 'why'

If they are going to make sense of their loss or trauma in a balanced and useful way, they first need to know what it is they are making sense of. The 'what' has to come before the 'how' and the 'why'. And then comes the 'therefore. . .', by which I mean: what are the implications of past events for the present and the future?

If the child does not have sufficient information about <u>what</u> actually happened and <u>why</u>, as they try to make sense of it they will search for things to fill in the gaps, and they might end up imagining things that are actually worse than the reality. Depending on the age of your child and what questions they have, they might not need each and every detail of events. But they will need a good-enough and comprehensive-enough account. And if they have specific questions, it's usually better to provide them with accurate and honest answers rather than leave it to their imaginations. Sometimes, you might be tempted to tone down the details to try to protect them from more upset. But they are likely to find out details at some point from others, or from the internet. It is much better to hear such details from you – a trusted and familiar adult who knows them well and can help them to make sense of things – rather than from someone that does not have their best interests at heart. You may choose not to give them all details at first, but it is better to provide them with a story that you can add details to as they get older or as they have more questions, rather than a story that you need to take away and replace with a wholly different one. It's a bit like a dot-to-dot drawing. For younger children you might just provide the outline of what happened, as they get a bit older or as they ask questions you start to join the dots with them, then later you could start to colour it in.

Nina, the six-year-old girl who had experienced her stepfather's violence towards her and her mother for several years, needed and wanted different amounts of information at different times in her life. When she and her mother first left her stepfather and went to a place of safety, Nina wanted to know what he had done this time that was different to all of the other times, and she wanted to know that he would not be able to find them. This helped her to feel safe at that time. But as she got older she started to worry about what he had done to her mother when she had not been there, and Nina started to imagine some really terrible things. Her mother answered all of Nina's questions about what he had done to her, including some nasty attacks. Nina had overheard some of the attacks from under her duvet, so if her mother had dodged those questions or minimised them, Nina would have known that she was not giving her a full account and so may well have imagined something worse. As Nina got even older, and started to have her own intimate relationships, she wanted to know *why* her stepfather had been so violent and whether all men were like that and whether she would have to marry someone like that.

However, you might not be able to control all of the information and the opinions that your child comes across. In addition to coverage by news and social media, which is covered in a later section, other children might be talking about it at school, or parents and carers at the school gate might be discussing it. Sometimes, people will come up to a child and start talking to them about it. It can be really helpful if you have been able to create an environment at home where things are 'talkable-about' and your child feels that they can ask questions, knowing that they will get an honest answer. Then if they do hear a different account of events from elsewhere, they are more likely to feel able to discuss it with you. That way you will have a better chance of knowing what they hear or read, and of helping them to make useful sense of it. For example, sometimes other people do not have the full story with all of the details, and they may fill in the gaps with inaccurate information. If your child hears such an account, you will want to know that, and want to be able to discuss what actually happened with them.

Your own thinking makes a difference

According to research, the way that your child makes sense of what happened is partly influenced by what those around them think about it, what they say about it, and what language they use.[29] Your thoughts and actions can influence your child's meaning-making, sometimes without even realising it. And their meaning-making can cause problems for them. So, if you yourself are struggling to make useful sense of events, it would be worth attending to your own thoughts and beliefs first. You might want to just talk it through with a trusted friend or colleague or you might prefer to get some professional support. This will be considered in more detail in the final part of the book.

Imagine a child overhearing their parent or carer speaking on the phone about an event – consider the different impact that the following two versions of the same event could make to the child and their meaning-making:

Negative meanings	Balanced meanings
Well, the storm and the flood were terrible. They've completely ruined everything.	*Well, the storm and the flood were terrible. The house will need a lot of work before we can go back, and some things we've lost for good; but we've managed to get some of the children's toys and a few of my bits.*
It was really scary because we didn't know if we would be OK. Even when the emergency services arrived in a boat, we weren't sure if we'd make it or not.	*It was really scary at the time, and even though it was still scary in the boat, at least we were on our way to safety.*
I don't think any of us will ever be the same, we'll never forget that night and how dangerous it was.	*I don't think any of us will ever be the same, we'll never forget how lucky we were to be rescued.*
The children are still struggling, they are so fragile now, they're afraid of everything.	*The children are still struggling, they seem to be a lot more anxious, but we're gradually doing more things. They were so brave that night, and we'll get through this together.*
We'd heard the weather forecast – we should have come to stay with you. I blame myself.	*We'd heard the weather forecast – I did think about coming to stay with you, but I didn't think it was going to be as bad as it was.*
The children haven't gone back to their swimming lessons. I don't really want them to, I think it's just easier to avoid things like that.	*The children haven't gone back to their swimming lessons yet. But the experience just highlights how important it is for them to be able to swim well.*
They're not back at school either. I'd rather have them at home with me and there's no hurry to get them back to school.	*They're not back at school yet. But we're going to work out the best way to do that, so that they can see their friends and get back on track.*

Note that the examples in the second column do not minimise what actually happened or its impact, but it does lead to a different conclusion based on the same facts.

Recalibrating and rebalancing beliefs

Of course, it's not always easy to help a child to see things differently, especially when trauma is involved. However, finding ways of viewing the experience from a more balanced perspective can have significant benefits for how your child makes sense of what has happened to them, and their world.

Offering lots of reassurance might help but might not actually address the core of the problem – their beliefs. It might be necessary to explore with them their beliefs and thoughts and help them to develop a more balanced way of thinking. This doesn't mean that you sit them down and have an intense conversation about what happened and what they think about it. It is better to provide opportunities to talk but no pressure to do so. Sometimes the opportunities present themselves very naturally, the trick is not to miss them when they do come up. It's useful simply to be curious and show an interest in their experience and what they make of things. Rather than feeling the need to 'correct' any unhelpful thoughts they may have, it can be more powerful to 'validate' and 'normalise' them. This gives them the message that they can be open with you and they are more likely to tell you more. You can then go on to help them to re-evaluate them. For example:

Child: I'm still too scared to go to bed on my own.

Carer: That sounds tough – tell me more, how come you're scared?

Child: What if we get burgled again?

Carer: I know that you're scared by what happened, and it makes complete sense that you would still be worried. It's very normal for people to stay scared for a bit after something like that. I'm really glad that you've told me about that. But tell me more, what do you think could happen?

Child: Well maybe that man or one of his friends could break into our house again and steal things, and what if I came downstairs to get a drink and bumped into him and what if he had a scary mask on, I saw a TV show, I think it was Scooby Doo, and the bad guy who was stealing something had a really scary mask on, and what if he tried to grab me.

Carer: That makes sense – I can see now why you're so scared. I think if I was thinking all of that I might be scared too.

And then, rather than discounting their logic by simply replacing it with your own, it can be really helpful to help them to discover their own new logic.

Carer: Do you think other people who live here are scared too?

Child: Well, you don't seem to be, and I don't think Esme [older sister] is either.

Carer: Oh, that's interesting. I think you're right. I'm not scared, and I don't think your sister is either – why do you think that is?

Child: Well she probably didn't watch that episode of Scooby Doo, and maybe you don't think we'll get burgled again.

Carer: Ah I see. Why would I not think we'll get burgled again?

Child: Well, you got new locks put on the door and you always check them when you come upstairs to bed.

Carer: Yes, that's true. Are there any other reasons that I might not be scared?

Child: Dunno.

Carer: Well, I guess I know how rare it is to get burgled and I don't think that they would try again – because I know that our neighbours and the police are all keeping a special eye out to make sure there is nobody around who shouldn't be. And yes, you're right, we do have very special new locks. Let's get the instructions out of the bin and read about how special they are . . . And you're also right that I am always careful to make sure that I lock the doors when I come in, and then I check them before I go to bed. That's why I'm not scared.

> I think your brain might still be scared because of when we got burgled – it can't forget it, and then it can't remember all about the locks and the police and everything. Maybe we need to help it to remember why there is no need to be that scared.

It can be very tempting to jump in with reassurance, but this can be counterproductive, and your child might end up feeling silly or undermined for the meanings they have made of the situation. And if you end up having an actual argument about their way of seeing things, then you may find that they cling to their views more tightly, when in fact you want them to start to loosen their grip. The above example shows how helpful it can be to keep being curious and keep asking questions..

Memories – not the whole story!

In Chapter 6, I explained how memories for traumatic events (which may include loss) tend to be different to memories for other events. And this can really undermine your child's sense of safety in various ways.

First of all, they may re-experience the fear associated with the actual event, so even if they are able to realise that it is not happening again, and even if they 'know' that they are safe, that is not how they *feel*. The child's sense of threat and fear remains current rather than in the past. Secondly, even after you have spent some time helping them to develop more balanced views, and they realise that they are safe enough, when those trauma memories intrude, the memories powerfully and repeatedly remind them of how unsafe the world is, how unsafe they are, and how others cannot be trusted to protect them. And finally, the fact that these vivid sensory-based memories can intrude into their minds in such a terrible way, however hard they try to ignore them or distract themselves, can make them feel that they don't even have control over what's going on inside them, let alone what goes on around them.

It may not be obvious that your child is experiencing intrusive memories, they might be working hard to try to avoid them, and they may worry that telling you about them will actually make them worse. So, you may need to do a bit of gentle detective work. It might be useful to make sure they know that having vivid volatile memories is quite common and understandable. You could use the cartoons in Chapter 6 to help to explain them.

Most of us would have some sort of intrusive memories or thoughts after difficult or distressing events. We may have a few nightmares over the following nights, we may find ourselves thinking about the events when we don't really want to, and we may suddenly recall what happened when we least expect it. But for many of us, the difficulties would settle down over the days and weeks that follow. We may start to talk about what happened with friends, we may write it down in an email to someone or in a diary, or we may just think it through on our own. All of these are ways that the memories become 'processed'. It's as if by thinking, talking, playing or writing about what happened we can change the <u>format</u> of the memory, so it becomes more like a story and more under our control. You can help your child with that same processing by:

- Reassuring them that such memories are understandable.

- Helping them to feel safe, because they are probably more able to think through what happened in the past when they feel safe enough.

- Not encouraging avoidance. If they want to talk about it, then even if it's difficult to hear, even if you or they get upset, don't close down the conversation. You may be afraid that it will make it worse, but it's much better for them to be talking it through with you when you can help them to feel safe, tell the story and process the memory, than it is for them to be thinking about it in an uncontrollable way, perhaps through intrusive images or nightmares.

If you have completed a formulation described in Chapter 9, not only might you have a clear understanding of why your child could be avoiding thinking about what happened, but also of how that avoidance keeps the problem going.

You might even provide opportunities to talk about it. You don't want to be forcing them to talk about it, but you do want them to know that they can tell you if and when they wish to. And if they do start to tell you about what happened, rather than avoid it, you can gently help them to tell the whole story. Try to:

- Be calm and comforting.

- Listen carefully and compassionately.

- Use your curiosity to help them to tell the complete story, all the way to the end, i.e. a moment when they were safe.

This approach will help your child to start to create the whole story in the right order. It will pull together their fragments of the worst moments but also the other facts, including that they got through it and are safe now. This process will help them to start to put the events behind them. Some children will want to use drawings or play to help them to tell the story. It's most helpful if you follow their lead rather than you force it on them.

If possible, try not to get 'over-involved'. That might seem like a ridiculous thing to say – your child may be traumatised by what happened, you may even have been traumatised too, how can anyone expect you not to be 'over-involved'? But as they start to tell the story, it's helpful if they have the clear impression that you can cope – both with the story and with their distress. You don't want them closing down in order to try to protect you. It's important that they get to tell their story, with your help and support, not that you simply give them your preferred version of events.

News media, social media and the internet

Where the traumatic event has been covered in the media, this can have the potential to be helpful, as long as it leads to a *better* understanding of the events. Even if it includes coverage of the worst moments of the events, some media accounts will include such moments within the context of the whole story, and this can ultimately help with processing the memories and making useful meaning of events.

But media (news or social) coverage that just goes over and over the very worst moments, that shows graphic images, that exaggerates the details, or is very unbalanced, is likely to be actively unhelpful. Helping your child develop a balanced understanding of the events, and thereby a reasonable view of themselves, the world and others, partly relies on how you understand the events, partly on the conversations that you have with them, partly on the conversations they have with others, and partly on what versions of the events they are accessing. It can be helpful to ensure that your child is accessing balanced versions and is aware of the positive things being done in response to events. For example, police efforts to catch and prosecute those responsible, actions taken by a community to come together and heal, or efforts to make things safer as a direct response to the traumatic event.

Dealing with different types of media is covered in more detail in Chapter 16.

Below is an abbreviated version of a form that you can use to help you to stop and think about your child's sense of safety. The full-length version is in Appendix One, and more copies can be downloaded from https://overcoming.co.uk/715/resources-to-download.

Quick post-trauma review – SAFE

From 0 to 5, how does your child's environment (the things, the people, the places around them), and their own resources and abilities support a sense of safety?

_____

What helps?

_____

_____

_____

_____

What ideas from the chapter that you have just read might you try to increase this further?

_____

_____

_____

_____

Key points

- Safety is the first principle and is about your child's actual safety as well as their 'felt' sense of safety.

- This starts by making sure basic needs are being met and putting in place some structure that provides routine, predictability and familiarity.

- Feeling safe also links to how they make sense of what has happened, and this is influenced by how others react. You can help them understand what happened in a balanced and realistic way.

- This might include helping them to process intrusive memories, by talking about, drawing about or playing about what happened.

- Depending on the circumstances of the trauma or loss, you might also need to manage your child's contact with news media, social media and the internet.

Feeling Calm and Harnessing Emotions

Part 1 described some of the different ways in which children may react to loss or traumatic events. It is completely normal for children to be upset or distressed immediately after such events. Their strong reactions are not necessarily a cause for concern. They might be very frightened, very angry, very sad. They might be agitated and find it difficult to settle. This is a completely understandable reaction and might even have been useful during the trauma.

In the early stages, rather than trying to stop their emotions, it might be more useful to let them express their emotions, with you there with them (if that's what they want). Have you ever opened a bottle of fizzy drink, only to find that someone had shaken the bottle up and suddenly the drink is spraying everywhere? If you try to push the top back on, you actually end up making it spray more and for longer, but if you let the spray out, then after a short while it stops spraying. Rather than trying to suppress your child's distress, what happens if you just sit with them and let them cry or be angry or whatever? That way they won't feel they have to hide their feelings from you and experience them on their own. They might feel embarrassed or ashamed about how they are feeling, or might even be scared by some of their reactions. If you are able to find out how they are doing (as described in Part 1), and then help them to see their strong reactions as a response to their loss or trauma, then they may feel less troubled by them. You could show them the graphs of the different paths and explain that lots and lots of children have high levels of distress and difficulties following such events. But over time, many of them recover, particularly those that have support to do so. Just because such reactions may be common, that does not mean that they should just be left to get on with it by themselves. Such reactions still warrant support from you.

Over the days and weeks that follow loss or trauma, many children will find it increasingly easy to be calm and their strong reactions will begin to fade. I described in Chapter 2 that it's a bit like putting a weight on to a set of kitchen scales. You put the weight on, the indicator goes up, you take the weight off and the indicator goes back to zero. Similarly if a child experiences a stressful or upsetting event, they have an emotional reaction but once the event has passed their arousal state returns to their resting state. But if you put a weight on that is too heavy, the scales may not return to zero. And if a child experiences a traumatic rather than a stressful event, even after the event, their arousal level may not return to their resting state straight away. As their carer, you can play a really important role in helping their arousal level to 'reboot' and return to its resting state.

If any sort of emotions are taking over and seem out of control, there are various things that you and your child can do to try to harness them. We're not trying to suppress or block the emotions – that often doesn't work. We're trying to regulate or harness them. Harnessing emotions is a bit like harnessing an excitable horse – the more somebody practices, the better they'll be at it. And the more you get to know the horse, the more you can get it to do what you want it to. Similarly, the more you and your child can practice taming their emotions, the more they'll be able to use them rather than be overwhelmed by them. And also like harnessing a horse, there are some 'drills' or exercises that can help your child to develop their skills.

Your role is a bit like that of a coach – you are there to help guide them, but you can't do it for them. And it's important to remember that sometimes they might need a bit of time on their own to use their strategies – if you find yourself running around after them shouting at them to use their breathing exercises, then that is unlikely to work.

Feeling safe – feeling calm

Feeling calm is obviously very closely linked to feeling safe, so the previous chapter about helping them to feel safe is really important. It may be particularly important to make sure that you have read Chapters 6 and 7 about memory and meaning.

After you

In the safety briefing in planes, they always tell passengers to fix their own oxygen mask before trying to help others. Similarly, if you really want to help your child to feel calm, then you need to get into a calm frame of mind yourself. If you are anxious, agitated or angry (possibly because of what your child is doing), then maybe you need to take a step away for a moment (if it's safe to do so), take a breath (or use some of the exercises described later in this section), and take some time to figure out what's going on for your child and what you can do to help support them. If you are not calm yourself, it's going to be really difficult to help them to be calm, and in fact they may even get more agitated. Ways that you can care for yourself so that you can best care for your child are covered in more detail in Part 5.

Psycho-education

To help your child feel calm, it can be useful to pick a moment when they are less distressed to help them to generally understand more about feelings and emotions, sometimes called 'psycho-education'. It will be difficult for your child to take this in when they are distressed, so wait until things are on more of an even keel. Explain to them that even strong emotions are not things to be scared of, they are completely natural, and can even be useful. They might have watched the Disney movie *Inside Out*, in which the different emotions drive different actions and all of them are useful at times: Anger helps to get things done,

Fear helps to keep the young person safe, Sadness helps to acknowledge a loss and move through it, Disgust prevents the young person from eating anything poisonous (or broccoli), and Joy helps the person to carry on feeling motivated. Any of these emotions can become problematic if they get out of control or overwhelming. For example, if Anger leads to getting into trouble at school, or falling out too much with friends, or if Fear prevented the person from doing *anything*, or if Disgust stopped them from eating anything other than pizza, or if Sadness made them not bother doing anything, or if Joy made them avoid anything that wasn't wholly fun which might make it difficult to get on with schoolwork, or to listen to friends who were having a hard time. So, the goal is not to avoid or suppress feelings, but harness them.

The importance of the right words – name it to tame it!

When a child is upset, I'm not sure that simply saying 'calm down' or 'don't worry' ever works. I do know that sometimes it winds them up even more.

One very basic way to help to harness emotions is to use words and language. Rather than just *experiencing* a feeling, help your child to *name* it. At first you might need to do it with them, or even for them, and then gradually encourage them to do it themselves. There is some important research that shows just how powerful labelling emotions can be – it actually changes what our brains do. In one study,

Professor Matthew Lieberman and colleagues found labelling emotions had a powerful impact on what happened inside people's brains in a way that other tasks did not.[30] The adults in their study had their brains scanned while pictures of faces showing different emotions were put on a TV screen in front of them. The amygdala is a part of the brain that is considered to be important in emotional reactions, and the brain scans showed that when faces showing emotions such as fear or anger were presented, the participant's amygdala was activated. The researchers found that various tasks such as matching the emotion to another face showing the same emotion, or labelling a first name that would match the gender of the face, made no difference to the activation of the amygdala. However, *labelling* the emotion that the face was showing activated parts of the brain in the prefrontal cortex (often thought of as the thinking part of the brain), which in turn seemed to dampen down the activity in the amygdala.

So rather than just telling them to do something that they probably would do if they could, you can start by using their name to get their attention, and then providing the words that describe what's going on. For example, instead of just saying 'I know how you feel,' you could say, 'Jack, I can see that you are really, really angry right now.' When you describe their feelings, use your face, your body and your tone of voice to mirror the feeling in a diluted form. So you might slightly tense up when you say 'really, really angry'. This shows your child that you've understood their feelings in a way that does not rely on language. Then show that you understand why, or that at least you are willing to try to understand. Rather than saying 'I know why', you might say, 'I know you were really keen to keep watching TV, but we have to go now, and I know how much you like that TV show.' This will help your child to feel understood, and providing words for their feelings when they cannot, may help to bring things back under control. However, it will be useful if you can also help your child themselves to learn to put their feelings into words rather than you always having to do it for them.

In practical terms this might mean having more everyday conversations about what your child felt rather than what they did, so that they develop their emotional vocabulary and are more used to labelling their own emotions. So rather than just saying, 'How was school, what did you do?' add other questions about their emotions such as, 'And how was that for you . . . ? Did you enjoy it . . . ? Did you find that challenging . . . ? What bits did you enjoy today . . . ? What bits did you least enjoy today . . . ?' You can also integrate discussions about emotions into other everyday conversations. If you watch a film together, rather than just talking about what happened, talk about how the characters may have felt and times that you and your child may have felt the same. On the way back from football, or after watching it on the TV, you could talk about the feelings of the players and the referee. Talk about how other people (on the news, or in films, or in sports) deal with difficult emotions.

Practical ways of working with emotions

There are also a number of practical exercises that can be done to help your child to calm. Difficult football skills need to be practised in training sessions, tricky steps in a dance need to be rehearsed before a performance, and complicated moves in a computer game need to be repeated before they can be done successfully. And it's the same with these skills for regulating emotions – if your child wants them to work when they actually need them, it's a good idea to practise them when the pressure is off. I've split these ideas into different groups: breath work, body work, head work and sensory work (or external stimuli). There are a lot of ideas here, and they won't all work for everyone, so you and your child might need to pick some to try and see how you get on.

Relaxation Strategies I – Breath work

When a child is not calm, their breathing often changes. As they get more anxious, or angry or excited, they start to take increasingly shallow and rapid breaths. Sometimes this can be frightening as they may feel as if it is difficult to catch their breath. If you did a formulation for your child as described in Chapter 9, you may have included your child's breathing as one of the physiological responses. And you may have noted how when their breathing changes, they start to feel more panicky. So for some children it is really helpful to support them to get their breathing back in line. There are different ways to do this, and you and your child can experiment to find out what works best for them.

Occasionally, breath work can increase panic, which makes breathing even worse, and leads to more panic. This makes it even more important that your child practises when they are calmer, and that you are able to get some feedback from them about how they find it. If the breathing exercises don't seem to work, just try some of the other techniques and let the breathing do its own thing.

With all of these, be sure to be careful about what your child with their specific experiences might make of the exercise. For example, a child who has been sexually abused may react if you, an adult, ask them to lie down and relax; or a child who has been with a parent as they took their last breath may react if you ask them to focus on slow breathing.

Belly breathing involves paying special attention to where the breath is going. This can best be done by encouraging your child to lie down somewhere comfortable and suggest that they focus on a spot on the ceiling or close their eyes, and start to notice their breathing. Don't try and change it, just notice it coming in and out. And then have your child place one hand on their chest and the other hand on their tummy and at first just noticing which hand is moving the most. Then, if it's not moving much, encourage them to breath deeper into their belly, so that the hand on their tummy is moving more than the one on their chest. Make sure they don't just lift their belly to make that hand move, we want them to notice that deeper breathes fill more of their lungs. The breathing needs to be natural and gentle, and not forced over-breathing.

Finger breathing involves tracing a finger from one hand up and down the fingers and thumb of the other hand, and breathing in as the tracing fingers goes up the other finger or thumb, and breathing out as the tracing finger goes down. This very simple technique helps your child to control and slow down their breathing. Depending on what suits your child best, you could start by having you trace your finger up and down their fingers and thumb while you both breathe in and out together. Then when they have got the hang of it, they could do the tracing themselves, possibly with you also tracing your fingers in time with them.

Breath counting is another approach that some children find useful. It involves counting while breathing. For example, they might breathe in while counting to five, pause briefly, and then breathe out for a count of five, briefly pause, etc. The actual numbers are not as important as the process of them focusing on gently controlling their breathing.

Relaxation strategies II – Body work

There are lots of relaxation guides for children available on the internet, or on apps. Many watches or phones have relaxation apps on them. Most of the relaxation exercises involve calmly helping the child to focus on their bodies and how they feel, and then noticing as their bodies relax and become looser and softer. Some might involve a 'body-scan' where the child shifts their focus smoothly from the top of their head slowly down to their toes (or the other way around). Others involve tensing different parts of their body and then relaxing them – this helps them to really notice the difference between tension and relaxation – something they may not have been able to notice before. There are some sample scripts in Appendix Two to guide you.

Some children find physical comfort from a trusted adult very soothing. Other children may find any sort of contact incredibly unsettling, and this may depend a bit on their histories and what has happened to them in the past. If they do find contact from you calming then you could try simple hugs, a hand massage, or a head massage. Even children that don't like other people touching them can sometimes find having something to play with helpful, for example small toys such as fidget spinners that allow them to be busy doing something, or things that are soft and tactile.

Some children find it really relaxing to be able to run around and burn off some of their nervous energy – that might be by playing sport or running around in the park.

Some children find it helpful to have a more objective measure of their physiological arousal level, to help them to notice what makes them more tense and what makes them more relaxed. It might be as simple as helping them to take their own pulse and seeing if they are able to lower it by relaxing, possibly by trying some of the breathing exercises above or other strategies described in this section. Increasingly it is becoming common for people to have devices such as watches or phones that claim to measure the wearer's stress level. This is a form of bio-feedback. Bio-feedback is a way of measuring something about the child's physiology which is presumed to be associated with their level of arousal – it might be their pulse rate, the variation between each heartbeat (known as heart rate variability or HRV), or skin conductance (which is a proxy for how open a person's skin pores are, which is associated with arousal). Some of these measures rely on being able to accurately measure heart rate and the time between the beats, but many watches and phones are not really able to do that accurately enough, so it's difficult to say exactly how accurate these devices are. However, I have worked with some children who really struggled to do a simple relaxation exercise but really engaged with bio-feedback which allowed them to check a number and try to reduce it.

Relaxation strategies III – Head work

It can also be helpful to teach your child how to calm their bodies by changing what is happening in their heads.

Special place is a technique that helps them to focus on something that helps them to calm down. You might need to help them to think of a place where they feel super-safe, calm, relaxed, chilled, stress-free, peaceful, laid-back, unperturbed, tranquil, serene, protected – whatever words work for you and them. This might be quite a challenging exercise if your child has never really felt safe or struggles to feel that. The place can be a real one, or a completely imagined one. Spend some time gently and calmly asking them for lots of details about the place: what can they see, hear, smell, feel, taste, touch? Is it warm or cold? Who else would be there with them? What would they be doing there? The more detail you can get them to create, the more vivid and the more powerful this exercise can be. If it helps, they could draw or paint their special place.

Then, perhaps with your help, they practise 'going' to their safe place in their minds and bringing to their attention lots of the details that they described earlier. After a bit of practice they can use it as a strategy whenever they need to feel calmer – they just remember what it's like to be in their place. In Appendix Two, I've included a script that you could use to do this exercise. But it's only there as a guide, don't feel restricted by it – do whatever is going to work best with your child. The idea is that by helping them to change what is going on in their minds, it will change what is going on in their bodies.

Music or stories (including audio recordings) can be very relaxing and soothing for some children. This might be partly because they distract them from whatever was troubling them. But there is an additional benefit for some children of the soothing tones or familiar voices and stories. If you have the equipment (e.g. a mobile phone) you could even record yourself reading your child's favourite story, or perhaps get a favourite member of the extended family to record one for them.

Worry time is a technique that involves scheduling time to worry. If your child is overwhelmed with worry about something and it's causing them a lot of distress or stopping them from doing things they want to do, you can tell them that you and they will think about this together later, you can set the actual time and place if that helps your child. This can communicate to your child that you are taking their worries really seriously. Then you can encourage them to get on with whatever it is that they want to be doing rather than worrying. Then of course it's important that when the allotted time comes, you remind them of your agreement to think about their worries together. You may find that often they no longer want to, or need to, think about them.

Most of these 'head-work' strategies involve an element of distraction, which can be really useful. But they don't just help the child at that particular moment, they also teach your child the useful lesson that emotions don't have to be feared and that they can harness them rather than being overwhelmed by them. However, they might not address the actual problem that is causing the distress in the first place, so if over time they are still needing to use the strategies regularly, you may need to spend some time getting to the bottom of their distress. If the difficulties have arisen because of their experiences of loss or trauma, then the sections of this chapter on meaning and memory may be particularly useful.

I explained in Chapter 6 how memories for traumatic events are different – they can be very vivid and often intrude into a child's mind. Such memories have a tendency to fill moments of silence and stillness. So, when doing the exercises above, it might be useful if your child can be quite occupied with the activities, rather than allowing too much 'space' for the trauma memories to intrude.

When your child manages their emotions successfully, make sure that you acknowledge that and celebrate it, e.g. 'I thought you dealt with that poor decision by the referee really well, you were clearly cross about it but rather than just mouth off at them you seemed to channel your anger into playing really well.'

Looking into the future

Given your child's experiences of loss or trauma, there are likely to be various things that they come across in their lives that may trigger strong emotions. One thing that can help them to manage that is to help them to anticipate them. If they are expecting the emotions to be triggered and if they can know when that might happen, they will be less surprised and more able to harness them. For example, lots of children's films cover death and trauma, some subjects at school may trigger particular thoughts or memories. There will also be some triggers that are less obvious and therefore may be more difficult to anticipate and prepare for. For example, simply being out of breath in a sports lesson might be an internal reminder of being breathless at the time of an attack, and this may trigger an anxiety response, or even a flashback. At times it might be better to avoid some of those triggers, but you don't want your child to rely on avoidance as their main strategy; it's far better for them to be able to anticipate the triggers and manage their reactions.

Self-harm and suicidality

Following loss and trauma, some children start to hurt themselves. They might start to bang their heads on things, they might pick at their skin until it bleeds and then keep picking at the scabs, they might hit or slap themselves, or they might cut themselves. This can obviously be extremely distressing for carers. But if you become aware that your child is hurting themselves, you won't be able to help them much if you yourself are too distressed. You won't be thinking straight, and your child may already be overwhelmed by their own emotions – they don't want to have to cope with anyone else's as well. So take a moment to think about how you are going to respond, rather than react.

Hurting themselves is not necessarily about wanting to end their life. Often it is a strategy to cope with their own overwhelming thoughts or emotions – the act of harm might distract them, or it might give them a moment of calm as their body responds to the harm, or they might be relieved to at least be in control of the pain rather than just experience the pain they feel following their loss or trauma. Other children harm themselves because they feel guilty about something that has happened and see the harm as punishment that they deserve.

Telling them to stop, letting them know how it upsets you, being cross with them, and telling them not to be so stupid are all common responses but are unlikely to help. However, there are things you can do that will help them to find other ways of coping.

Talking with them can help – but don't rush in with solutions or fixes. As mentioned earlier in the book, it's important to listen calmly and carefully. You can be gently curious to find out more and open up conversations rather than close them down with your own ideas. But don't make it into an interrogation. Resist any desire to 'get to the bottom of it', your role here is to listen and understand, then your child is likely to tell you more. You know your child better than anyone else, so you will know when they have had enough of talking. Try to go at their pace and don't feel that you have to solve everything in one go. It can be helpful to focus on the thoughts and feelings behind the self-harm, rather than the actions. As they tell you things, try to let them know that you've heard and understood what they are saying. And if you haven't understood, then ask gentle questions to find out more. You can let them know how normal it is to feel very strong emotions. They may be 'catastrophising', which means that they may think that everything in their life is terrible and nothing will ever go right for them. You can help them to have a more balanced view by helping them to see their strengths and successes.

They may find it really embarrassing or distressing to tell you about acts of self-harm, so don't push too hard for details; it might be more useful to find out what support they would find helpful in the future.

There are some practical things that you can do too. If they are cutting themselves, you can start by removing things such as knives that children might use to hurt themselves with. It's difficult to make it impossible for them to harm themselves, but if you can make it more difficult then there is more of a chance that the urge will decrease before they actually do anything. You can suggest some less harmful strategies that might help. For example, you could suggest that they hold an ice cube firmly against their skin; this will provide them with strong physical sensations without doing the physical harm. There may be other things that you can help them to think about doing that will distract them when they are feeling like self-harming such as changing their location, or using some of the strategies described earlier in this chapter. These strategies don't usually stop self-harm completely, but they might help some of the time. You could also provide them with some of the details for accessing additional support contained in Appendix Three, which they could access themselves.

When they are so distressed that they are contemplating self-harm, they probably are not able to think about the various strategies and other sources of support that they might have discussed with you. So it can be useful to make an actual 'safety plan' with them. This simply lists all the different things that they can do when they feel over-whelmed with distress. It can be written down and kept somewhere for them to refer to when they need to.

Suicidal thoughts, suicide attempts and completed suicide are all rare in pre-teen children, but they do happen, and children from about the age of eight understand the concept of suicide and are capable of carrying it out. Creating the best environment for recovery as described throughout this book is likely to reduce the risks, but it is important to do your best to ensure that your child is able to talk to you about their feelings if they want to, and they will know that you will listen to them without judging them. If they do mention wanting to take their life, or wanting to be dead, it's important to take this seriously. If you are worried that there is an actual immediate risk then treat it as an emergency and take them to an Accident and Emergency Department or call 999. Otherwise the advice in this chapter is relevant when it comes to suicidal thoughts.

If your child is self-harming or feeling suicidal, I recommend that you get some additional support. Your GP or family doctor is often a good place to start. Appendix Three includes details of some additional resources. You may also be finding it difficult to cope, and Part 5 is all about how to make sure that you are supported.

Social support

Sometimes, it's enough for a child simply to have someone else there with them. Simply being with someone, preferably someone that they know, love and trust, can be enough for strong emotions that are overwhelming them to settle down. The next chapter may impact on feeling calm, because it is about how to help your child feel supported and connected.

Below is an abbreviated version of a form that you can use to help you to stop and think about your child's sense of calmness. The full-length version is in Appendix One, and more copies can be downloaded from https://overcoming. co.uk/715/resources-to-download.

Quick Post-trauma Review – Calm

From 0 to 5, how does your child's environment (the things, the people, the places) and their abilities support a sense of calmness?

_____

What helps?

_____

_____

_____

_____

What ideas from the section that you have just read might you try, to increase this further?

_____

_____

_____

_____

Key points

- Feeling calm is closely linked to feeling safe, as discussed in the previous chapter.

- What your child knows about the event, and the space they are given to experience their emotions about it can support feelings of calmness.

- Practical strategies such as different types of relaxation can support calmness.

- Suicidal thoughts or self-harm may be a result of feeling overwhelmed. As well as the support suggested in this chapter it is important that you seek some additional support in such situations.

Feeling Socially Supported and Connected

Most children, even those that find relationships difficult, do better when they feel connected to, and supported by, others. Generally, a child who feels they have an attachment to a loving and caring adult will be more likely to be able to cope with difficulties. And this is even more important when it comes to dealing with loss and trauma. That sense of being connected can be very comforting, even if the person to whom they feel connected is not present. This feeling connected and supported is one thing that may help your child recover and get through a loss or trauma. When we analysed lots of research to understand which children were more likely to have PTSD, we found that children who felt less supported and those that isolated themselves were more likely to have PTSD and their PTSD tended to be worse.[31]

Often, following loss and trauma, children can feel isolated and on their own. This can be for various reasons. Some people who would ordinarily have been a source of support, such as friends, family and neighbours, may not know what to say after loss or trauma, they may even worry that they will say the 'wrong thing', and they may fear making things worse. And so they avoid the child altogether. Eight-year-old Seb was run over, and his parents told me that friends and family actively avoided them all – neighbours would cross the street to avoid them and extended family stopped calling because they were all worried about what to say.

Some children will deliberately isolate themselves after loss or trauma and deliberately avoid contact even with people they know well. This might be because they are worried they will get upset in front of others and are embarrassed about that. Other children avoid contact with others because they are worried they will be asked questions about what happened, and they don't want to have to talk about it. And still others avoid contact because they are worried about upsetting other people. This means that just at the time that they need support from others more than ever, they have to manage without.

There is some interesting research which shows that if a friend is close by, not so close that they can see or hear what is going on, then adults tend to rate hills as being less steep.[32] At first I thought this research was a bit trivial, but the more I think about it, the more I think it's amazing that the availability of social support will change how you see things. But the researchers went on to do a second experiment and they found that just bringing a friend to mind will make them see the hill as less steep, compared to thinking about someone who is not a friend. So, even if they are not physically available, just bringing to mind someone to whom you have a positive connection makes a difference to how you see things. There is also some research that shows that holding someone's hand changes the way that your brain reacts to an adverse situation, and that effect is stronger if the person is someone you know, love and trust, although it still makes a bit of a difference even if it's someone you've only just met.[33]

Strengthening your child's connections

So, social support and connection is important, and can help following loss and trauma – but often that's just when children find themselves, or make themselves, more isolated. You can help your child, by ensuring they are as supported and connected as they want to be. You could think about your own role but also the role of others (such as friends, extended family, school staff, neighbours, etc.) in providing support and connection.

If your child has experienced loss or trauma, then it's even more important that you are available to them. Of course that doesn't mean that you drop everything and are 'on call' 24/7 just in case they want to speak to you. But it can be useful to set aside some extra time, so that you can have some uninterrupted time together – it doesn't have to be 'special time' to do something particularly deep and meaningful, it can be something pretty mundane that you can share. It's the quality of the connection rather than the activity that is important here. So, if you're sat on the sofa next to them watching a movie, try to resist the temptation to use your phone to catch up on some important communication or jobs, but just focus on being with them and sharing the same experience (I realise this might be challenging if they are keen on watching something that you find especially annoying – but maybe you could find a compromise),

If the loss or trauma has also affected you, think carefully about how you are doing and where you are going to get your support from. Having a carer who is open about how they are doing can be really helpful for children because it sort of gives them permission to talk about how they are doing too. Having a carer who is struggling with their own grief and trauma and so is completely unavailable is not so helpful for children. You may need to spend a bit of time helping yourself, so that you can best help your child. I'll talk about this more in Part 5.

You could also bring in some other people such as friends and family with whom your child has a connection. There may be some members of the family that are not very local, but you could still help to strengthen your child's connection with them. Perhaps they could send letters, pictures, video messages to each other. This will help your child to realise that there are people out there who are on their side, with whom they have a connection, and who are thinking of them. And this enhanced connection not only reduces the chances of them feeling isolated, but it can also strengthen your child as they get through any difficulties.

As well as the support they receive from you, try to notice if they are having less to do with their friends, dropping out of activities with peers, avoiding other people, or just spending more time on their own. Your child may need a bit of additional encouragement to make use of their normal sources of social support. You may find that you have to be a bit more proactive setting up playdates, and be a bit more involved in getting them to and from places than usual. Obviously, you don't want them to feel that you are trying to palm them off on to others, because their connection with you and the support you can provide is also really important. Equally, you don't want to force them into something that they really not ready for. But they might just need a bit of help from you for a while to get up and running.

You could spend some time with them 'mapping out' their social support network. You could do this as an activity together. One way would be to encourage them to draw a small picture of themselves in the middle of a sheet of paper, or just write their name. And then draw two or three circles around them of different sizes. Then ask them about all the important people in their life and get them to place each person somewhere in the circles to indicate how important they are to them, or how close they feel to them (you may need to explain to younger children what 'feeling close' means, and how it is different to actually being close to them).

Make this as playful and fun as you can. Your child could use buttons, Lego figures, Lego blocks, toy animals, stones,

Post-it notes with names or drawings on, to represent each person. Don't worry too much about what they choose to represent each person, what you're interested in is where they place them. You can then follow this up with some questions to find out who provides them with what type of support:

- Who would you want to go to if you hurt yourself, e.g. if you fell over and hurt your knee?

- Who is good to have around if you feel sad about something?

- Who can help you if you feel worried?

- Who makes you feel strong and confident?

- Who helps you to do things?

- Who do you help and in what ways?

- Who could help you fix something that was broken?

- Who do you wish you could spend more time with?

- When you look at your map of your friendships, what do you reckon – is it about right, or would you like to make some changes? Add some other people, move anyone in closer, move anyone out a bit?

A more playful way to do something like this is to think about different islands. One island is where your child lives. A second island is joined by a bridge, and your child has the key to the gate on the bridge, so they can let people from the second island onto their island, and your child can also decide when to go and visit people that live on the second island. A third island is separated from the first two islands by shark-infested waters. Then encourage your child to think about the people in their life (family, friends, neighbours, teachers, etc). As in the first exercise above, your child could use buttons, Lego figures, Lego blocks, toy animals, stones, Post-it notes with names or drawings on, to represent each person. Then ask them where they would like to place them. As they are thinking about where to place each person, talk with them about what sort of support they offer to your child.

If your child does seem to be having less to do with you, family or friends, it might be worth trying to work out why that might be. As explained in Part 1, thinking about memories and meanings can help to understand what is going on for children after traumatic events. For example, a child might stop having contact with their friends, if visiting their house involves doing something that triggers a traumatic memory (e.g. walking past a certain place or getting on a bus). Remember that traumatic memories are so easily triggered that there only has to be a small amount of similarity between the trigger and the actual event to trigger the memory. It might be a house that has a similar front door, or a café that emits a similar smell, or the friend's parent might remind them of somebody. Or has the traumatic event changed the way they see themselves, the world or others? Do they now see themselves as worthless and think that friends would not want to spend time with them? Do they believe that the world is unsafe and so feel safer staying at home? Do they consider that other people are untrustworthy, and so to prevent them from being hurt again they think it's better to stay away from everyone?

The easiest way to understand what is stopping your child from accessing their normal sources of social support is to gently ask them. And ask them what it would take to help them. They may need help to process the memories of what happened, or they may need help to rebalance their views of themselves, the world and others.

Connection to the person that died

What if one of your child's strongest connections was to a person that has died? The impact on your child is likely to be more intense. But the person's death does not mean that the connection needs to be severed or minimised. As mentioned in Chapter 8, maintaining a connection to the person that has died is very often useful. Sometimes the adults around the child worry that dwelling on the past will get in the way of them moving on, but often going through the pain of grief and developing an ongoing connection is actually part of moving forwards. Some children like to have a physical object that reminds them of the person that died. It might be something that belonged to them like a watch or a piece of jewellery, or it might be something that the child created since the person died. Perhaps a picture they drew, a photograph of a treasured memory, or something that represents things about the person that died to help the child remember them.

Many child bereavement services help children to make salt-sculptures – a small jar full of layers of different coloured salt, in which each layer represents something about the person that died. For example, there may be a blue layer that represents the person's eyes, a yellow layer to represent a treasured memory of a trip to the beach, a green layer to represent how calm and kind the person was, a brown layer to represent the fact that they always used to give them chocolate, etc. It's a good idea to plan out the different colours first. Not only will the salt sculpture act as a physical memento for the child, creating it provides lots of opportunities to discuss the person that died and strengthen the ongoing connection. First, find a small glass jar with a lid that you can use. A jam jar might be too big and will probably use too much salt, so you might prefer to find something smaller. Then, fill the jar with table salt – this will help you to work out how much salt you need for the whole thing. Now it's time to decide how many layers of different colours the child wants, and write down on a piece of paper what each colour represents. Spread out on the table a piece of paper for each layer, divide the salt from the jar onto the pieces of paper. For each piece of paper, rub a coloured chalk into the salt until the salt is coloured the way that your child wants it. Then, one sheet of paper at a time, carefully pour the salt into the jar. Give the jar a gentle tap between each layer, so that it settles and does not move too much after it's finished. The layers don't have to all be level, you can create patterns by tilting the jar as you pour the salt in. When you have finished, if there is any room at the top, pour in more salt until it is very full. Finally, put the top in and glue or tape it down.

Some children also love to have a memory box – this is a box (e.g. a shoe box) that contains various things that remind them of the person that died such as a tie, an item of clothing, photographs, jewellery, perfume, toys, etc. The child can then use their salt sculpture and memory box to remind them of the person whenever they want to. This dipping into the past can really help them to move into the future.

Below is an abbreviated version of a form that you can use to help you to stop and think about your child's sense of social support and connectedness. The full-length version is in Appendix One, and more copies can be downloaded from https://overcoming.co.uk/715/resources-to-download.

Quick Post-trauma Review – Social Support and Connection

From 0 to 5, how does your child's environment (the things, the people, the places) and their abilities support a sense of social support and connections?

_____

What helps?

_____

_____

_____

_____

What ideas from the section that you have just read might you try, to increase this further?

_____

_____

_____

_____

Key points

- Feeling socially supported and connected is important, and can help following loss and trauma, but often that's just when children can become more isolated.

- Understanding if your child's social network needs boosting, and 'mapping out' their social support network can be helpful.

- If your child has experienced the loss of someone close to them, they may need some support in helping them remain connected to the person who has died.

14

Feeling in Control

Self-efficacy

When we talk here about 'feeling in control', it's not quite as simple as having choices and being able to make decisions, although that is part of it. It's more about a sense of 'self-efficacy', which means that your child has confidence in their ability to influence things around them in a positive way. It's more than simply feeling that you have some control over things, it means believing that you have control over some things and that you can use that control to solve problems that will have a positive impact on your life and wellbeing. Research has found self-efficacy supports wellbeing and recovery.[34] But as with many of the other principles mentioned here, although it is related to how well children cope following loss and trauma, it is one of the things that has most likely been compromised or damaged by their loss or trauma. Following the loss or trauma, your child may feel that they have no control over anything that happens around them, or even worse, they may feel that what happened was their fault i.e. that they did have control, and yet it still happened.

Memories and meaning-making

In Part 2, I described how important the meaning that your child makes of the loss or trauma is. Some children see themselves as having no influence over what goes on around them even before a loss or trauma and they do not believe that they can really do much about their life. So, the loss or trauma simply confirms those beliefs. Others may start off with a sense that they are in control of things and can do things to influence what goes on around them. But then the loss or trauma gives them the very strong 'message' that they are powerless and cannot influence things. Children may have tried really hard to stop the loss or trauma, but it happened anyway. This just confirms the notion that they are powerless. They may start to believe that they are weak or a failure because they couldn't stop the events from happening. They then approach things with a 'CAN'T-DO' attitude, and this may mean that they don't bother trying. This in turn means that they don't have many successes, which then just confirms their view of themselves as weak or failing. You may have identified similar patterns if you completed the formulation in Chapter 9. You may have been able to identify how your child's loss or trauma coloured the way that they see the world, themselves or others. And this then results in certain thoughts, feelings and actions, which may actually keep the problems going.

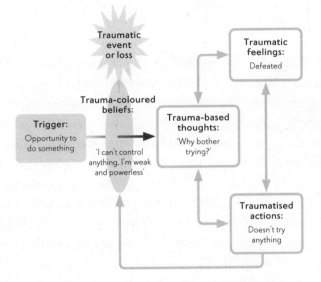

The memories of the loss or trauma may act to re-enforce their views. For example, they might try hard to get back to school, and when a peer asks them about what happened, their memory of the trauma or loss, and importantly the sense of powerlessness, are activated very strongly, which just reminds them that they can't do things. So they go home early, which just confirms that they can't cope. The intrusive nature of their memories, and their inability to prevent it from intruding may also contribute to their ideas that they cannot control things – because they cannot even control what happens inside their own minds.

Repairing or rebooting your child's sense of self-efficacy

As their carer, you are really well placed to help your child to see things differently. This might mean finding a way to interrupt the cycle described above, such as helping them to have successes, even mini ones, and then helping them to notice how they are able to influence things around them. Or there may be other ways that you can help by repairing their self-confidence so that it is as strong as it was before the loss or trauma, or it might be a case of re-booting it. One way of thinking about this is to provide them with plenty of 'evidence' that undermines their sense that they can't do things successfully and points to how much control they do have. This can start to make the idea that they <u>can</u> do things that lead to a positive impact for them increasingly irrefutable. There are a number of ways that you can try to do this.

Choices

The first is to help them to see that they do have some control over some things that go on around them. How can you help them to feel that they can influence what happens, and not that things just happen around them and to them?

Simple steps like giving them some realistic choices might start to repair their confidence in their ability to influence things. Of course, there will be limits to what they can control, and it's important to be honest and transparent about this, so that their expectations are managed. It can also be frightening for children if they feel that there are no limits and that they can do whatever they like. Keeping boundaries and limits in place is one of the things that will help your child to feel safe and that life hasn't completely changed. So, they may not be able to choose if or when they have their tea, and there may be a limit to the choices they can have about their food, but they might be able to choose between peas or sweetcorn, and where they sit and whether they have their tea before or after they get into their pyjamas.

I'm not suggesting that simply providing choices over small things will magically heal your child's trauma, only that it begins to bolster their view of the world where they do have some choice and control.

Mastery experiences

You can also help them to have multiple experiences which demonstrate their ability to successfully solve problems and overcome obstacles. Initially this might include some relatively minor accomplishments so that they experience some success before moving on to more challenging tasks. You could help them to overcome current difficulties, for example they may be finding it really difficult to get back to school, and you could support them to do that in small manageable steps that will have plenty of 'successes' built in rather than expecting them to do things too quickly. You will of course want to help and support them, but be a little careful. Particularly after loss and trauma, it can be really tempting to do lots of things *for* your child, because of 'what they've been through'. But think about this carefully – you don't want to give the impression that you think they can't manage. Quite the opposite – you want to give very clear messages that they absolutely CAN do things, and that they can do things that will have a positive impact on themselves. But they might benefit from support with that, and you certainly don't want them to feel abandoned and unsupported. I'm making it sound like it's a really difficult balancing act – but it isn't. You don't have to over-think it and get it perfect every time. It's about considering how you can make sure that they have enough support to be able to do things, but not so much support that they feel disempowered. For example, following a loss, if there is a funeral or some sort of memorial being planned, how can your child take an active role in that, what decisions can they be involved in?

Positive messages of belief – implicit and explicit

In addition to experiences of being successful, you can also bolster their confidence with implicit and explicit messages of your belief in them. Explicit messages might be as simple as you telling them that you know they can do something and giving them encouragement. Implicit messages might be you demonstrating through your actions that you believe they can manage things successfully rather than doing everything for them.

Role models, family members, and superheroes

You can also help by drawing on examples of other people who have the ability to successfully overcome challenges and influence things for their own benefit. This might be family members or friends, sports personalities that you and your child both know about, or characters from films. For example, most superheroes have overcome significant trauma during their childhood – many of them experienced traumatic bereavements. But with the help and support of loving and nurturing carers, they were each able to overcome their challenges and become superheroes.

Lee had had an extremely traumatic childhood but was then adopted by an amazing carer. When he was ten years old, he explained to me how superheroes and villains all have experienced childhood trauma, but the superheroes had all subsequently been cared for by loving and nurturing carers. In one of our sessions, he wondered with me whether that care made the difference between them becoming heroes or villains. Given the trauma and traumatic losses that superheroes have experienced, you may be able to draw parallels between superheroes and your child, not just in terms of their experiences, but also their attributes (e.g. courage, determination) and their ability to influence things around them.

Children who believe that they are no good at anything, and believe they can't do anything, often forget times that they have succeeded. As described earlier, the beliefs they have about themselves act as a lens, which then filters out information from the past that does not fit with their negative view of themselves, or colours information so that it does fit. This means that they may find it easier to remember the times that they have failed, or when things have not gone their way. Or when things have gone well, they focus on the negative aspects. So, it can be useful to remind them of those times that they have successfully overcome challenges. There may even be stories about them when they were very young which they don't remember at all which can be shared with them as a way to remind them about their strength and courage.

Harnessing emotions

As described in Part 1, and then explained in Part 2, after trauma or loss, some children will struggle with strong emotions. This can make them feel as if they have no control or influence over what is going *inside* of them, let alone what is going on around them. This can confirm beliefs they might have about themselves as powerless. So, helping them to gain some mastery over their own feelings, as described in the previous section can challenge their ideas about lack of self-efficacy and help them to feel in control of their body and the feelings rather than the other way around.

Managing expectations

Following loss or trauma, some children will feel that their worlds are suddenly very unpredictable and uncontrollable. You can help to repair their view of their world by reducing the number of surprises they encounter. If you are going to have to collect them early from school for a dental appointment, make sure that they know this in advance, otherwise the sudden change of plan for them may really throw them. You might think that telling them they are going to the dentist will upset them, so it can be tempting to keep the information from them until the last possible minute, but following loss and trauma one of the things that you will want to repair is their sense of control, and springing things on them at the last minute may not help.

Managing the approach of other adults around them

As their parent or carer, you can also play a key role in ensuring that the other adults around them are empowering and enabling them, rather than undermining their confidence. Of course, you want your child to be well-supported but that does not mean that they need everything done for them – that risks simply adding to their sense that they are useless and powerless. It might be necessary for you to speak to other adults in your child's life, such as teachers, family members, neighbours, therapists, etc., to ensure that they understand the importance of offering support in a way that empowers the child rather them undermines their confidence.

Below is an abbreviated version of a form that you can use to help you to stop and think about your child's sense of control and self-efficacy. The full-length version is in Appendix One, and more copies can be downloaded from https://overcoming.co.uk/715/resources-to-download.

Quick Post–trauma Review – In Control

From 0 to 5, how does your child's environment (the things, the people, the places) and their abilities support a sense of feeling in control?

_____

What helps?

_____

_____

_____

_____

What ideas from the section that you have just read might you try, to increase this further?

_____

_____

_____

_____

Key points

- Following the loss or trauma, your child may feel that they have no control over what happens around them, or that what happened was their fault.

- You can help to repair your child's sense of control by giving them realistic choices about some things that go on around them, helping them have mastery experiences, and bolstering their confidence with implicit and explicit messages of your belief in them.

- Examples from others who have overcome challenges can provide role models for your child, be they family members, friends, superheroes or celebrities.

15

Feeling Hopeful

It's important to remember that being optimistic and hopeful about the future does NOT mean minimising what has happened or trying to railroad your child to think positively. However, research does show that people who are able to remain optimistic despite their experiences of loss and trauma tend to have a better recovery.[35]

As discussed earlier, for some children the loss or trauma changes the way they see themselves, the world and others. As a direct result of their experiences (including those before the loss or trauma), some may start to believe that:

• They are powerless and cannot change anything that happens to them

• They will not be able to cope

• Bad things will happen to them routinely.

Some will focus on the catastrophic aspects of everything, and some will find it impossible to see any sort of positive future for themselves. Such beliefs are a fertile breeding ground for hopelessness and despair.

Clinging to a certain amount of hope about their future seems to protect children from the loss or trauma completely shattering their views of themselves, the world and others. You can help your child to remain hopeful. As described in the previous section, you can help them to see themselves as able to cope and able to affect things around them.

Actively avoiding talking about the past is unlikely to be helpful, but you can help to keep their focus balanced between the past, the present and the future. Without trying to distract them from the past, you could ask them about their plans for the future, or what they will be doing in one year's time, or what they are looking forward to in the next six months, or even just the next two weeks.

There may even be opportunities to ask if there is anything that they have learned from their experience of loss and trauma that will actually help them in the future – what have they learned about themselves, what have they learned that will help them to tackle future challenges? Of course, you will want to pick your moments carefully. It might make things worse if you try to have such conversations when they are having a panic attack, or when they are sobbing their hearts out, or when they are being really angry. But when they are calmer and in a more reflective mood, you could ask them what strengths and abilities they have that are helping them to cope with their current difficulties. This will also help you to assess their level of hopelessness. If you completed the formulation mentioned in Chapter 9, you may be aware of how their loss or trauma may have coloured the way they see themselves to such an extent that it obscures their view of their strengths and abilities. Without stretching the truth, you can help them to remember or to notice their strengths. This might include their social support – you can remind them about their good friends who are supportive.

If they are experiencing some of the difficulties described in Part 1, they may well be feeling that their experiences have had some lasting damaging effect and that they are unable to cope with future challenges. It can be useful to talk openly about their psychological reactions and help them to see that these are understandable reactions to what happened, they are not signs that they are not coping or that they cannot cope. You can also help them to see that there are things that can be done to help them with their recovery and help them to get through this difficult time. If things are a bit better this week than they were last week, then it may be useful to help them to see this. Sometimes children can be so preoccupied with their difficulties they are unable to see the subtle improvements. Noticing any improvements that might have occurred can help them to realise things are shifting. But it's important to balance that with the knowledge that recovery is rarely a straight line, and that things are likely to go up and down. So, if things are a bit worse this week than last week, that doesn't mean things are deteriorating; it may just be part of the natural up and down of the road to recovery.

Try not to dismiss any worries about the future too quickly. Saying 'oh don't worry about that', or 'everything will be fine' is unlikely to help. It might make them feel that you do not want to hear about what is going on for them and then they may keep their worries to themselves in the future.

By remaining curious and open you can help them to get their worries about their futures out into the open. Sometimes the simple act of saying things out loud can help them to see if they are unbalanced and unrealistic. Also once they are out in the open and can be talked about, you can gently help them to develop a more balanced view. If they have particularly catastrophic or exaggerated thoughts, it can be helpful to acknowledge that such thoughts or views about things are understandable given their experiences, but you can also gently counter those thoughts with facts – not in a way that leads to an argument or leads to them shutting down, but in a way that helps them re-evaluate things.

Below is an abbreviated version of a form that you can use to help you to stop and think about your child's sense of hopefulness. The full-length version is in Appendix One, and more copies can be downloaded from https://overcoming.co.uk/715/resources-to-download.

Quick Post-trauma Review – Hopefulness

From 0 to 5, how does your child's environment (the things, the people, the places) and their abilities support a sense of hopefulness?

_____

What helps?

_____

_____

_____

_____

What ideas from the section that you have just read might you try, to increase this further?

_____

_____

_____

_____

Key points

- Being optimistic and hopeful about the future does NOT mean minimising what has happened or trying to railroad your child to think positively.

- But it is important to support a sense of hope.

- Simple strategies such as gently asking about their plans for the future, or what they will be doing in one year's time, or even in just the next two weeks, can help build feelings of hope.

16

Responding to the Media, the Police and the Courts

News media and social media accounts

News media and social media have the potential to help children understand traumatic events in a useful way. Such accounts may, in theory, help them to form a truthful and useful view of the world and the associated risks, and they might help them to think through what happened so that their memories are processed and stored as a complete narrative rather than as the original sensory data.

But sometimes, news media and social media focus on the most striking moments, possibly going over them time and time again, rather than providing children with the big picture and the whole story. Amateur footage and personal accounts are often made available in an unedited form through social media. The people providing the descriptions and images of events on news or social media may not be so interested in accuracy, they may be more interested in getting as many views or 'likes' as they can. And sometimes such accounts become very popular.

This 'social rumination' tends to emphasise the message of how dangerous the world is and how vulnerable children are, rather than focusing on how rare these events are, what actually happened and why, or why the world is generally still safe enough.

Repeated exposure to graphic images and spectacular emotional accounts of the very worst moments, without a balanced and accurate commentary to accompany it, obviously increases the risk of traumatisation. This can be because the child's focus is repeatedly drawn to the worst moments of the incident, rather than to the explanation behind it. Some research studies have shown a link between repeatedly watching media versions of events and the subsequent development of lasting psychological difficulties.[36] It is possible that this is because children who have the most difficulties are most in need of an explanation of events and so they tend to watch more media coverage in the hope of making sense of it. Nevertheless, it seems more likely that the repeated watching of videos or reading of spectacular accounts, makes things worse.

Other people around your child may have been watching those videos or reading such accounts. So even if your child has not come across them directly, they may well hear of them from other sources and then they may be curious to see them for themselves.

This means that it can be helpful if, as much as is possible, you are aware of what media your child is accessing.

It is also helpful if you can support your child with the accounts that they come across. You may be able to restrict their access to such unhelpful accounts, particularly for younger children, but as they get older that becomes more difficult. Some aspects of the event may remain accessible on the internet indefinitely, so your child may well come across them at some point as they get older and have more independent access to the internet.

However, you can help your child make sense of such accounts and digest them, rather than try to simply prevent them from coming across them. You can help by talking about media accounts (social and news) openly with them so that they know that they can discuss them with you. There may be certain accounts that they are highly likely to come across, for example if there was a high profile criminal case that was reported widely by the news media, or if there has been a TV documentary made about the event. In such cases, you may even want to be proactive and go through the account with them – this way at least they will be coming across it with you to assist them rather than on their own at some point.

Noah, Judith and Seth were three siblings aged seven, nine and twelve when their father was killed as his car crashed off the motorway into a bridge. There was extensive news coverage of the incident, including some graphic video footage of the crash site clearly showing the crumpled car.

Their mother knew that all three of them would probably come across those images from the news at some point, so rather than it happen unexpectedly when she was not there, she decided to record the news coverage, check it herself and then watch it with all three of the children. It was very upsetting for all of them, but she would rather the children watched it with her present to support them and explain it, than they saw it on their own, or at a friend's house. There was some additional amateur video footage of the crash scene as the police and ambulance arrived that was available on a social media site that twelve-year-old Seth might have come across unexpectedly. So she decided to also watch that with just Seth – she did not think the younger children would come across it and decided to see if it was still available when they were old enough to use that particular site.

The more that you and your child are able to communicate openly about what they are watching and reading, the more likely you are to know what they are accessing, and the more that you can help them make useful sense of the information and the images that they come across. If they know that you will tell them the truth and answer their questions honestly, then they will know that you have given them an accurate account, so when they come across exaggerated or inaccurate versions, they will know that that is the case. You might even be able to help them notice the impact that accessing media accounts has on them and assist them in reducing their access themselves.

Dealing with media intrusion

If your child was directly involved in an event that is of media interest, you may find that your child becomes part of the story that is being reported, and you may find that media want to talk to you and your child directly. You may want your child's story to be told accurately, but once you give information to media outlets you have no control over that information or how it may be presented to tell the story the media wants to tell, rather than the story that your child wants to be told.

If you and/or your child do decide to talk to the media, there are some tips that will help you manage it.

- Ask the reporter what the purpose of the story is and the content. Find out what story they are wanting to tell and how your input will fit into it.

- Think in advance what you are and are not happy to talk about. There might be limits on what you are happy to have shared, and it is helpful to decide what those limits are beforehand, and then stick rigidly to them. It's easy to add more information afterwards. It is impossible to take information back once it has been shared.

- Some journalists are expert at making people feel so comfortable that they end up sharing much more than they intended to, and much more than they wish they had done. You can make sure that the reporter knows what the limits are – it might not stop them from asking, but it might help you to feel more comfortable saying, 'As I told you earlier, I'm not prepared to talk about that.'

- Decide whether it's a good idea to involve your child directly or not. And be clear with the reporter about your decision. If you decide to involve them, then make sure that you support them before, during and after. Help your child to realise that they do not have to answer a question if they do not want to. This can sometimes be difficult, because children are used to being asked questions at school or by you, and usually they are expected to answer every question, but this is a different type of interaction. They should feel free to stop the interview at any time they wish, and you may need to support them with that. Don't be afraid to intervene if necessary. It's better to interrupt too early to ensure that interview goes in the right direction than once something has been said that cannot be unsaid.

- You may want to make sure that the reporter has worked with children in the past, and you could even read some of the other stories that they have written to get a sense of their approach.

- After the interview, discuss it with your child, ask them if they are worried about anything, and be sure to prepare them before the final story is released.

- Make sure they realise that the reporter and editor might make a lot of changes to the story, and you and your child's input may only form a small part of the story – and it could even be edited out completely.

Coping with police investigation and prosecution including court cases

Some potentially traumatic events will lead to a police investigation and subsequent prosecution.

The process of the investigation can be difficult and distressing. You may be tempted to try to protect your child from it completely, and prefer the police not to investigate. However, it actually has the potential to help your child's recovery.

Police investigations and meaning making

The police's investigation might find out exactly what happened. This can help a child to understand events, and perhaps help them to understand *why* it happened, which can help them make sense of things in a balanced way. For example, if a child is cycling to school and suddenly a car coming the other direction swerves right across the road and knocks them off their bike, in addition to having to recover from their physical injuries, they might be psychologically traumatised by that event. As well as traumatic memories of the event, the child's meaning-making may be part of the ongoing difficulties: if cars can swerve to the wrong side of the road so unpredictably, then the whole world may seem completely unpredictable and unsafe.

However, the police investigation might discover that the driver was reaching down to the car floor to retrieve their mobile phone. This information helps to explain (not excuse) the event. It could help the child to realise that most drivers would not reach down to the floor while they were driving, and then the child can regain a more balanced and realistic view that the world is safe enough and fit the event into that view.

The investigation is also important because it may lead to a criminal prosecution, and this also has the potential to assist in your child's recovery. For some children, a world in which such events can happen can be terrifying and change their view of the world as a safe and predictable place. But the world can seem less frightening and random if the person that caused the event is held to account, goes to court and has to deal with consequences (such as a prison sentence, a fine, or no longer able to work in certain jobs, go to certain places, or have contact with certain people). Furthermore, if your child is actually able to contribute to the investigation and prosecution, for example by helping the police and possibly giving evidence at court, then although the event might have made the child feel power-less and out of control, playing a role in the prosecution could help them to regain some sense of control.

The challenges with police investigations and court cases

However, the investigation and court case can be really difficult, and you are in a crucial position to be able to help and support your child through this. It can be useful to have a sense of what difficulties you and your child may face to help manage expectations:

- The careful collection of evidence may take some time. This process can be frustrating, and many children and families feel that they cannot begin to 'put the event behind them' until the investigation has been completed. But the police's job is not just to find out what happened and whether a crime has been committed. They have to gather evidence in a very particular way so that a jury is convinced by it.

- Police interviews can be a long, drawn-out process. It may involve repeated meetings with the police and your child. They may be asked to go through the event many times, possibly in the unfamiliar surroundings of an interview suite. However, the interviews are usually conducted by specially trained police officers who will go out of their way to make the process as gentle as possible for your child. Occasionally, in some areas, the interviews may be completed by mental health professionals who have been trained by the police to be able to conduct inter-views that collect the required information in a way that will survive the scrutiny of the court process. You can help and support your child through this process by making sure that those conducting the interviews know information about your child that might be useful. Because of your expert knowledge of your child, you can also help the investigators to understand when your child has had enough in a particular interview and needs a rest, or needs to continue on another occasion.

- The investigation might not result in a criminal prosecution, which could be very upsetting for your child. They might worry that the police did not believe them, or feel that they have been let down. This can make the world seem really unfair and that they are not valued by others because what happened to them has not been taken seriously. You can support your child by helping them to understand that the decision about whether or not to prosecute someone is not a reflection of whether they were believed, and is not related to whether or not they are valued. It can be helpful to explain to them that in order to prosecute, there must be a reasonable chance of the prosecution being successful in the court. This may depend on all sorts of factors such as whether a jury can be convinced of the person's guilt 'beyond reasonable doubt', and depending on the strength of the evidence, that might be difficult to achieve.

- Your child might need to give evidence in the court, which could be considered to be quite an ordeal. Depending on which country the court is in, there may be a variety of 'special measures' that can be used to try to support children in giving evidence. For example, your child may be able to give evidence by video link or have a screen in the court room, so they do not have to see the defendant. Your child should be able to visit the court room or the room from which they will give evidence in advance so that they can become familiar with it. Someone should explain to them the procedure, who will be asking questions and in what order. Sometimes an 'intermediary' might be used to assess your child and then give the court clear guidelines about the nature of the questions that they can be asked.

- Some cases attract media interest, which means that after the court hearing, details might be available, and not only will your child have access to those details, so will other people that know your child, such as friends and parents of other children at the school. The details could include the account given by the defendant about what happened and why, and this might be distressing for your child. In such cases, the previous section on managing media intrusion may be particularly helpful.

- The court might not return the verdict that your child would like, and any sentence may not be in keeping with your child's expectations. Your child may be preoccupied with the result and could be very upset if they are not happy with it. You might need to help your child understand how a court works and the limitations in its decision-making processes.

Don't be afraid to consider all options when helping your child make useful sense of the event, the court hearing and the outcome. For example, I have worked with many children who have had one parent go to prison for killing the other parent, and much to many people's surprise, it can be useful for the child to visit the guilty parent in prison. If carefully managed, this may provide an opportunity for the child to receive an apology, and to hear sufficient details of what happened and why, to help them make sense of the event.

Key points

- In addition to the actual event, other factors such as police or media involvement can help or hinder recovery.

- Planning ahead how you might handle the media, police investigations and court room appearances can be vital.

- Keeping in mind the Five Principles can help you in supporting your child to feel safe, calm, connected to others, in control and hopeful.

17

Choosing Your Child's 'Team'

As your child's carer, you are obviously in a prime position to support them with their recovery following loss or trauma. But you should not feel that you have sole responsibility for this. There can be a team that can help, with you as the 'manager'. Team members might include neighbours, friends, family members, professionals (such as teachers, social workers, therapists, support workers, sports coaches, activity leaders, GPs, etc). It might be a small team (perhaps just you and a teacher), or it might be quite big. The first trick is to pick a good team – you will want to surround your child with people who are able to help your child's recovery. Given the Five Principles we have just covered, you are likely to want to include some people who are:

- Consistent, reliable, balanced and stable – this will help your child to feel <u>safe</u>.

- Comforting and reassuring – this will help your child to feel <u>calm</u>.

- Friendly and warm – this will help your child to feel supported and <u>connected.</u>

- Collaborative and empowering – this will help your child to feel <u>in control.</u>

- Optimistic and cheerful – this will help your child to feel <u>hopeful.</u>

You may struggle to find people who can tick all of those boxes, but that's why you have a team – so that different people can fulfil different roles. Do you have any ideas about who could be on the team, or already is?

The next trick is to try to ensure that the team are working together well. That might mean you have to ensure that different members of the team are communicating with each other, and they all have enough information for them to be able to support your child to the best of their ability within their particular role. Sharing this book might help them to share a similar understanding of what is going on, and what can help.

In Chapter 11, I mentioned how useful it can be for your child to be able to talk through what happened and what they think of it. They might choose to do this with you. However, they may find that difficult – they could be worried about upsetting you, or that they will be in trouble for something, so they might prefer to talk about it outside of the home with someone that they are not going to see a lot of the time. Don't feel bad if that's what they choose to do – let them know that you are happy for them to talk about it (if they want to) to anyone that is going to be useful. There may be some occasions when you will want to help them to make good decisions about whom to speak to – sometimes their peers are the best at listening – sometimes they are not.

Nina, the six-year-old girl who had experienced her stepfather's violence towards her and her mother for several years, would sit in lessons and was very good at paying attention to lots of things that she perceived (wrongly) to be potential threats, rather than to what the teachers were saying. The teacher, talking about the eight times table, was unlikely to be considered a threat and therefore, in Nina's mind, was not prioritised for paying attention to. The teacher noticed Nina paying attention to everything apart from the content of the lesson. This frustrated him, he raised his voice and spoke to her quite harshly as he walked towards her. Nina, who was already in a heightened state of arousal, saw an angry adult male, raising his voice and walking towards her. This triggered her stress response and she lashed out physically at the teacher, who was taken by surprise and defended himself. This event sparked a response by the school, which meant that all her teachers started to pay more attention to her, which in turn increased the pressure she felt, and this meant she found it even harder to pay attention to the content of lessons, and lashed out more frequently.

Initially her difficulties were thought to be due to Attention Deficit Hyperactivity Disorder (ADHD). But eventually, as her carer continued to help the professionals around her see the link with the trauma, she was correctly diagnosed with PTSD and received the appropriate and useful support. The therapist from a local charity offered therapy, which included her carer in some but not all of the sessions. Being included in some sessions meant that the therapist had a full picture of how Nina was doing at home, it meant that the carer could support her in the sessions and also meant that the carer could see how to talk with Nina about the trauma in a useful way.

Key points

- You are in a prime position to support your child's recovery following loss or trauma but you should not feel that you have sole responsibility for this.

- Recruiting other team members can help both you and your child.

- Try to involve people who are reliable, comforting, friendly, warm, empowering, and hopeful.

18

Recovery and Moving Forwards

It's worth remembering that the road to recovery is unlikely to be a straight path. There will be particular times where it may seem that things have got worse again, but that might just be a blip along the way. The dual processing model of grief suggests that children dip in and out of their grief as they move forward and adjust to their loss, so in fact those occasional increases in difficulties are likely to be part of the journey. Some of the blips may be predictable, e.g. at anniversaries or other significant events; others may appear to be out of the blue. So, if things seem to have taken a turn for the worse, don't just assume that things are going backwards, or that any improvement has evaporated. Stop and reflect. Try to work out what has caused the change, and think again about what might help – which might include reaching out to other services as necessary.

Preparing for anticipated events

Sometimes, there is advance warning of future potentially traumatic events. For example, a family member may have a terminal diagnosis, or your child's illness may require a significant medical intervention. This gives you an opportunity to prepare your child for what is to come. The timing can be important – if you tell them about it months in advance they may ruminate on it and imagine the very worst outcomes, but if you tell them just a few minutes before they may feel very out of control and may resent you for not telling them sooner. You know your child well and are in the best position to make a well-informed decision about when to start telling them. It can be helpful to share your ideas with another adult just to check that your plans seem sensible. You may need to return to talking about the future event or events several times, as your child may have different questions and they start to make sense of the information that you have shared with them. It can be useful to ensure that your child knows that it is OK to talk about the event and ask questions. Your response to their concerns and questions needs to be calm, containing, honest, accurate and appropriate. Don't be afraid to buy yourself sometime by saying that you will answer a question, but you just want to find out some more information, or consider how best to answer it in the most useful way.

Should you be worried?

Spontaneous recovery is common

In the graph showing different 'trajectories' or paths referred to at the beginning of the book, it is worth noting that most studies have found that more children follow the 'recovery' path than the 'chronic' path. That means that it is completely normal, understandable and possibly even healthy to experience distress and difficulties after certain particularly upsetting events. But for very many children those difficulties settle down over the days and weeks after the event.

Identifying children that need additional help

But, even with the best help and support from those around them, some children do develop difficulties that warrant extra help from professional services. There are no clear-cut tests to work out which children need additional help and which don't. But here are some things to consider to help you work out if you should be seeking additional professional help:

Severity
How serious are the difficulties?
E.g. Do they feel a little low or do they feel utterly despondent and hopeless?

Duration
How long do the difficulties last?
E.g. If they lose their temper, do they get over it in a few minutes, or does it last all day?

Frequency
How often does it happen?
E.g. Is it a bad dream every few weeks, or every night?

Change
Broadly speaking, are things getting better, worse or staying the same?
E.g. If you had a graph, which way would the trend be going?

Impact
How much of a problem does it cause and in how many different parts of their life?
E.g. Does it stop them from doing things that they would like to?

Persistence
How long have things been going on for?
E.g. Is it just a couple of days or several months?

What should you do if you are worried?

Family doctors or General Practitioners (GPs) can be helpful in helping you work out how concerning problems are, and then making appropriate referrals to support services if necessary. Also in the UK, many NHS Child and Adolescent Mental Health Services (CAMHS) have helplines you can call. There has also been a huge increase in mental health support available through schools, and it is likely that your child's school will either be able to provide some additional support or will know where to turn.

You can also contact various organisations to discuss your concerns and see if there is additional help or support that can be provided. Details of possible sources of additional support are included in Appendix Three.

If you think that additional help is necessary, and you are able to access some, don't be afraid to check out exactly what that help consists of, how it works, and what is involved.

And finally . . . Post-traumatic growth

This book has been about how to promote recovery and reduce problems for your child if they have experienced potentially traumatic events. But it is worth knowing that there is a body of research that has studied *positive* changes that come about because of traumatic events. This is not to say that any positives outweigh the negatives, but that research repeatedly finds that people often report some positive changes following traumatic events, not just negative ones.[37] These are usually in three specific areas:

- Self-perception – a child might feel stronger because they have gone through a challenging experience.

- Relationships with others – children might feel closer to relatives and friends, or they may value their relationships more.

- Attitude to life – a child might develop a different view of what is important in their life.

You are in a key position to help your child to find some positives. However, you will need to do it in a way that doesn't simply try to replace their negative meanings with positive ones, as that approach is likely to backfire and close down communication. Children may feel that you are trying to minimise the event or its impact on them if you try to help them find benefits. But it is possible to start to identify some positive meanings you and your child can weave into the meaning making process. In particular, you can build on pre-existing strengths and ways of seeing the world that would be considered to be positive. While we have focused so much on what goes wrong and how to minimise that, it is important not to overlook any positive changes!

Key points

- Recovery is rarely straightforward and there will be times when things seem to have gone backwards, but this might just be a blip along the way.

- Some of the blips may be predictable, e.g. at anniversaries or other significant events; others may appear to be out of the blue.

- If things seem to have taken a turn for the worse, don't just assume that things are going backwards, or that any improvement has evaporated.

- Do try to work out what has caused the change and what might help, using the tools in this book.

- Do consider reaching out to other services as necessary.

PART IV

◇◇◇◇◇◇◇◇◇◇◇◇◇

Specific Types of Events

I will now consider specific types of events, the particular ways that those events can cause difficulties, and how the Five Principles Approach might be used to guide the responses of those around the child. It will be more helpful to read these in addition to the explanation of the Five Principles, as otherwise these examples might not make much sense.

The Five Principles outlined in previous chapters are helpful after any potentially traumatic event or loss but there may be certain things to bear in mind or ways to apply them depending on the type of event. And although there will be some examples of how those principles can be put into practice, you know your child so will be able to choose how to apply them in your particular situation.

Finally, if the child that you are caring for has experienced traumatic events that are not specifically described below, you may find it useful to read the sections that are most similar to their experience to see how the approach explains the possible impact of the events and what might help.

19

Individual, single-event trauma

These are one-off events that affect a single individual or just a small number of individuals, rather than events that are repeated or chronic and affect whole groups.

Witnessing or experiencing physical assault and interpersonal violence

There are certain things about interpersonal violence that make it particularly toxic from a psychological point of view. To be directly confronted with the simple fact that someone has deliberately done something to hurt a fellow human-being can be quite difficult for anyone to get their head around, especially if it was not expected. Earlier in the book, I gave the example of a physical assault changing the way that a child might see themselves and the world. Experiencing or witnessing violence can leave a child with the belief that nowhere is safe, that any person has the capacity to be violent, and that they themselves are defenceless.

As described earlier, the memories of the assault may become traumatic memories. Those memories may be very distressing as they intrude into the child's consciousness of their own volition and can be very vivid. The child may even re-experience the physical pain of the assault. The child understandably may try to push that memory away, resulting in the memory remaining unprocessed. If the assailant was known to the child, they may start to question their own ability to make accurate judgements of other people's character, and blame themselves. This might result in them withdrawing from social contact in case they make the same mistake again.

Sometimes it is not the assault or the violence itself that is the cause of the trauma, it is the reaction of other people. For example, if adults around at the time were unable to do anything to stop the violence, then the trauma may not be the assault itself but the disappointment in the lack of action of others. The child may come to believe that their friends or carers are not what they thought they were. The child might then start to question not just their friends and family, but also their own worth and value, or their ability to make sound judgments about people.

Initially, helping your child to feel safe might involve being with them as they leave the safety of their home. But if you do that every time, then there is a risk of re-enforcing certain unhelpful and unbalanced beliefs such as *the world is too dangerous for me to go out alone* or *people are violent*. So, encouraging and supporting your child to gradually return to their previous level of independence can actually over time help them to feel safer and more confident in their ability. For example, if you gradually encourage and enable your child to travel independently to a friend that lives nearby, not only would you be actually helping them to feel safer in the longer term, you would also be drawing on some of the other principles. You would be encouraging their social connections and support, you would be increasing their sense of control and 'agency', and you might be helping them to feel more hopeful about their future being one full of doing and achieving things with others, rather than one with very little in it. All of this will help set the scene for their recovery. The formulation described in Chapter 9 might help you to understand what sorts of beliefs your child has developed about the world, other people and themselves. For example, they might have started to believe that *everywhere* is dangerous *all of the time*, rather than just that place at that time. As well as helping them to overcome their avoidant coping, it can be useful to also help them to develop more balanced beliefs. You can help them to do this by talking with them about how they see things and starting to point out exceptions to their traumatic view. For example, helping them to notice all the places that are safe and all the people that are not dangerous. This is best done gently and collaboratively. If it becomes a heated argument about whether their views are right or not, your child is unlikely to change them.

Traffic crash

Beyond the basic 'physics' of a traffic crash, and the basic 'biology' of any injuries, there are various qualities of such events that may add to the potential for the event

to be traumatic. Sometimes it can take a while for the rescue services to get a person out of the car. Many of them
will have seen films where cars that crash then explode
into flames, so to be stuck there waiting to be freed can
be terrifying. And if the child is able to get out but their
carer or someone else is stuck in the vehicle, then that can
be just as terrifying. I worked with one girl who was in a
car crash; everyone assumed that the moment of impact
must have been the worst moment for her, but in fact the
most distressing aspect of the crash was when she was sat
in the ambulance while the rescue services were using all
sorts of noisy machinery to cut the car and then peel the
metal back in order to get her mother out. When I met her
several months later, she could not stop imagining how
scared her mother must have been – it was the memory
of THAT moment that was intrusive and distressing.
Even after the crash, children may have to be taken by
an ambulance to hospital. All of this can be frightening,
and the experience may involve substantial pain too.
Children may have to return to the hospital for follow-
up appointments which might trigger memories of the
original event.

An additional difficulty might be that it is almost impossible in most countries to avoid getting close to cars, which
mean that there are plenty of triggers for any traumatic
memories. These multiple triggers may prompt the fear
associated with the original event, and then over time the
fear reaction becomes generalised and associated with
all traffic situations and not just the crash. If the child

experiences this repeatedly and each time gets away from the situation quickly, it means that the association between traffic and the fear is strengthened. They are not able to get used to traffic and their fear does not decrease.

There could be a belief (which might be true) that the crash could have been avoided, if only someone had done something different. If it is someone else that could have done something different, the child might feel extremely angry towards them. And if that person is someone the child knows, and maybe even loves, it can be extremely confusing and complicated for them to navigate the complex mixture of feelings. They might not feel 'allowed' to blame the person, so they may not talk about their feelings. By not talking about their feelings they deny themselves the opportunity to express them and have some help in making sense of what happened. If the child believes that *they* could have done something differently, they may feel incredibly guilty about the event.

As explained in the section above about meaning, the meaning that the child makes of any event is crucial in determining how they will react. The following are all meanings that some children have made of traffic crashes:

- Another crash could happen at any time.

- Bad things happen – especially to me.

- I am fragile because of my injuries.

- Other people cannot be trusted to keep me safe.

If such beliefs are short-lived, they may not have too much impact on the child, but if after weeks the child still has such unhelpful beliefs, it's highly likely that they will lead to problems. In order to 're-calibrate' these beliefs, it can be useful to use a combination of actions and words. The actions might be to gradually encourage and support them to return to travelling in the car or walking on the pavement next to increasingly busy roads. It can be helpful to do this very gradually. It's better to go slowly rather than too fast. So, if they are not ready to travel in the car, they could just sit in the car until they feel less anxious. Then they might sit in the car and imagine travelling in it. The words might involve talking with them about their fears and their assumptions, and helping them to develop more balanced and useful ideas and expectations.

Helping your child to develop more balanced and useful beliefs can be an important part of helping them to feel safe, calm connected, in control and hopeful.

Of course, in reality many of these events might not actually be isolated single events. A physical assault may come after a period of bullying or harassment and might not be the most traumatic event. Similarly, a road crash could lead to lasting injuries, and the injuries and medical intervention required might add to the trauma, or even become the most traumatic aspects. It is therefore important to consider a single event within its broader context of other events to understand the meaning.

Traumatic Bereavement

Not all bereavements are actually traumatic. Some may be very sad, and even tragic, but still not traumatic. A traumatic bereavement is when there is something about the nature of the way the person died which gets in the way of the normal grieving described earlier in this book. Children who have been traumatically bereaved may be so affected by the death itself, that they cannot start grieving their loss.

Traumatic Memories

For example, if someone that a child loves dies in a car crash, then rather than being sad about their loss and remembering the good times they had while the deceased was alive, the child may be stuck on being scared about the death itself. If they were present, they may have intrusive traumatic memories, or even if they were not there, they may be suffering from intrusive images of what they imagine happened. So, any time somebody encourages them to think about the person that died, or tries to help them with their grief, in fact it is the child's traumatic memory or image that is triggered. It's as if they are too scared to be sad.

You can help them to change the format of their traumatic memories or images, by allowing them to talk about the death if they want to. You can listen and support them as they start to take the images and sensations of their experience and create the story of what happened. This 'processing' will not make the death any less sad, but it can help the memory to be stored in a different way, so that it is less intrusive and less frightening. This is described in more detail in Chapter 11.

Meaning-making

As described in earlier sections of this book about trauma, the death may shatter their assumptions about the world, themselves, and others. For example, if the death is the result of homicide, a bereaved child might come to believe that the whole world is very unsafe, that they are vulnerable and that other people are violent. As a result, they might find it impossible to trust other people and they may start to withdraw from friends, family members and others. So, just at the time that they could benefit more than ever from social support and connection, they become increasingly isolated. Completing a formulation as described in Chapter 9 might help you to notice where their difficulties come from, and how their actions may be maintaining the problems.

They might believe that the death was in some way their fault, or that they should have stopped it. In these cases, they may need some help to get these beliefs out in the open and start to think them through more rationally. You can assist with this by gently discussing their thoughts and beliefs. As mentioned elsewhere, the trick is to not rush in with your own thoughts and beliefs in the hope that your child will suddenly change their ideas. It is better to support your child to reach their own new, more balanced, more helpful logic. You can give a clear message about your beliefs, but allow your child to come to their own conclusions rather than force yours on them. For example, you might say, 'I see now that you think it was your fault, and I can sort of understand how you would think that. But I really want you to know that I do not think it was your fault, not even a little bit. I think it was the fault of the person who killed him. They knew what they were doing, and they chose to do that. They could have chosen to do something else, but they didn't.'

If the death was the result of an illness, a bereaved child may become preoccupied with illness and their own symptoms, wondering if they also have an illness that will lead to their death. Again, you can help them by taking their concerns seriously enough so that they will talk to you about them. Then you can help them to realise how rare the disease was, how they are now paying much more attention to their bodies than they used to, and so they are spotting all sorts of bodily sensations that previously they would not have noticed.

Being bereaved by suicide understandably throws up lots more obstacles to a child's grief. In addition to the manner of the death, which may have been violent or sudden, there is also the meaning that the child might make of it. Some children see a death by suicide as an active decision on the part of the person that died to not be with them. They might consider this to be the ultimate act of rejection and make them feel unloved and even unlovable. Some children will feel guilty and wonder, if they had been better behaved, or if they hadn't had an argument, whether the person would still have taken their own life.

Again, you can help your child to think these things through more logically, in a more balanced and more helpful way. It can be useful to explain that many people who take their own lives may not have been thinking straight: they might have thought that there was no hope for things to get better and thought that suicide was the only way to stop feeling so bad. Or they could have wrongly thought that people would be better off without them. You can help your child to realise that the person who took their own life may not have been thinking about the impact on everyone they were leaving behind, they might have just been feeling so bad that they couldn't think of anything other than how to make their bad feelings stop. You might be worried that your child will try to take their own life too. And in fact they might also be worried that they could end up doing the same thing.

If they start to talk about wanting to be with the person that has died, of course take this seriously, but don't panic. Try to find out a bit more about what they mean – do they actually want to die too, or do they just really, really miss the person that died and simply want to be with them again. If it seems that your child does want to die, then see Chapter 12 for further advice; but it is important to reach out for additional help, for example from your family doctor or GP.

If your child is worried that they might end up taking their own life if they struggle with overwhelming feelings, make sure that they are aware of all the different strategies they can use to cope, and ensure that they have a number of people (including yourself) that they should contact if they do start to feel overwhelmed.

Key points

- Individual single traumatic events are those that are a one-off and do not affect whole groups of people.

- In supporting recovery from individual trauma, it will be helpful to consider how you can understand your child's experience of that trauma using the approaches outlined earlier in this book, and how you could apply the Five Principles.

- Consider the event in the context of other events (that might not have been traumatic) to help understand what the event actually means to your child.

20

Complex Trauma

The term 'Complex Trauma' means traumatic events that are caused by a person or people, and that are repeated or persistent rather than a single event.

Bullying (physical, verbal, cyber-bullying)

Bullying is when someone does something repeatedly in order to hurt someone else emotionally or physically, or in order to get them to do something. In this section, I am going to focus on the impact of bullying by other children or peers. Such acts committed by adults who should be caring for children will be covered in a separate section below about physical and emotional abuse.

Bullying is surprisingly common. The UNESCO Institute for Statistics estimates that around the world, on average about one third of children have been bullied.[38]

Despite being relatively commonplace, this does not lessen the potential impact on individuals. Because bullying is often a repeated act it can increase the psychological impact because it makes it impossible to write it off as a single event, and it can make the child dread parts of their daily routine. Bullying can very easily lead to an ongoing sense of threat – not just something that has happened in the past, but something that could happen again. Children who are bullied might start to avoid places or people rather than risk being exposed to further bullying. Although this might prevent a further act of bullying, avoidance could perpetuate the child's belief that the bullying will happen and may have a number of other 'costs' for them, for example they might miss out on important positive experiences such as education and social contact.

Sometimes bullying involves threats rather than actual violence, which might make the child being bullied reluctant to tell other people in case they minimise it or in case they do not do anything about it. Not only does this mean the bullying does not stop, it also makes the child feel that they have no control over things that are happening to them. Some ideas about what can help:

- Make the bullying 'talkable about'. Try to create an environment where your child can tell you about what is going on.

- If they do start to talk, try not to jump in too quickly trying to solve it or sort it out.

- Remain curious and ask questions about how they are feeling, or how they have been coping with that.

- Try to resist moving straight into 'problem-solving' mode.

- If the bullying is ongoing, then obviously this needs to be addressed first. You can't help your child to *feel* safe if they *are not* safe.

- When addressing the bullying, look for opportunities to empower your child and build their confidence. If you just go and sort it out for them, then there is a risk that that might knock their confidence; they might feel even less in control and more vulnerable because you did everything on their behalf. I do appreciate how difficult this can be! When something like bullying happens to your child, it can trigger a very basic emotional response! You might understandably feel angry or outraged, and you may well want to go and sort it out. In the final part of the book, I will discuss how you can take a breath and manage your own responses so that you can provide the best chance for your child to cope with their experiences.

- Discuss with your child what they think would help, and how you and they can work as a team to address it. That might mean that you call the school but that you and your child attend a meeting with the headteacher together. In this way you are empowering your child and supporting them to address the problem rather than doing it for them and taking even more control away from them. Of course this is something of a balancing act – you don't want them to feel that you are deserting them and leaving them to sort it out for themselves, but neither do you want to add to their feelings that they have no control.

There might be other ways that you can help your child to cope with bullying and you can discuss different strategies for dealing with it. You could list ALL the possible tactics, with the mantra being 'no idea is a bad idea'. Then you can go through each idea, thinking about what they might actually involve and what effect that might have on the situation. Many parents and carers start to look into self-defence, some form of martial arts training, or even boxing classes. These might be one aspect of a useful approach, particularly if the classes are likely to increase your child's self-confidence and give them some tools to be able to defend themselves if bullying does happen again. But if they end up encouraging your child to be more aggressive themselves, or if they are seen as a way to go out and reap revenge, then they are unlikely to be useful and will most likely lead to more incidents rather than fewer.

If the bullying is in the past and not an actual current threat, and your child is now withdrawn, anxious, low or angry, then you can help them to manage their thoughts, feelings and actions. By having conversations with your child where you remain in 'curious investigator' mode rather than as fixer or advice-giver, you can start to help them bring their thoughts and beliefs out into the open where they will be more able to re-evaluate things. They might be stuck in that avoidance cycle where they have a frightening thought about being bullied again, and because that upsets them they push that thought away. Or they might think that past bullying means that they are weak and power-less. Whereas if you can help them to think those thoughts through, they are more likely to be able to reassess things, recalibrate their thoughts and develop more balanced beliefs. But you can also help them with strategies mentioned earlier in this book for managing their feelings.

This could include helping your child to reassess their beliefs more accurately so that they feel safe, which is the first principle mentioned earlier in Part 3. Helping them to find some strategies to regulate their emotions can enable them to feel calm (the second principle). And if you can support them to start to reconnect with their peers then you will also be attending to the third principle of connectedness and social support. As they start to regain their confidence they might feel they have more control over what is going on around them (fourth principle) and will also start to see a brighter future for themselves (fifth principle).

Physical, emotional, and domestic abuse

According to the National Society for the Prevention of Cruelty to Children (NSPCC):

- Physical abuse is when someone physically hurts or harms a child on purpose.

- Emotional abuse is when someone repeatedly mistreats a child emotionally (e.g. deliberately scaring, humiliating or ignoring a child).

- Domestic abuse is 'any type of controlling, coercive, threatening behaviour, violence or abuse between people who are, or who have been in a relationship'.

An NSPCC study which surveyed young adults in the UK about their experiences before the age of eighteen[39] found that:

- 12 per cent had experienced physical abuse.

- 7 per cent had experienced emotional abuse.

- 24 per cent had been exposed to domestic abuse between adults in their home.

Studies in the US that were collated by Professor Merrick and colleagues surveyed adults about their experience of adverse childhood experiences (ACEs).[40] It used a different survey to the NSPCC study mentioned above, so we can't really make direct comparisons. But it found that:

- 18 per cent had experienced physical abuse.

- 34 per cent had experienced emotional abuse.

- 18 per cent had been exposed to domestic abuse between adults in their home.

Physical, emotional and domestic abuse are probably more common than those figures suggest because some of the people that answered the questions may have not wanted to share that information. And the US study did not ask about threats or controlling behaviour, which can also be so damaging for children and would be described as domestic abuse.

In this section, I am going to focus on abuse that is perpetrated by someone that is in a caring role, such as parent or carer.

These forms of abuse can have a significant impact on children, even if they are not directly involved in it. In Chapter 7, I mentioned that traumatic events that happen between people (interpersonal) tend on average to be more psychologically toxic or damaging than a non-interpersonal one. But it can be even more harmful for a child if the traumatic events happen in their home, and if the person responsible for the act is not just another person, but a person who is supposed to be caring for them. Most children have carers that they can trust to look after them, to protect them from physical and emotional harm, and support them when something upsetting happens. Children learn to rely on their carers, and as they get older they are gradually able to become less dependent on them, safe in the knowledge that their carers will be there if they need them. In this way, children can develop a view of the world as safe enough, of others as trustworthy enough, and of themselves as worthy enough. But with domestic abuse, the very people who are supposed to offer that care and support are the ones that are responsible for physical or emotional harm, which can have a catastrophic impact on children and change the way they see the world.

These types of abuse are usually not single one-off events, they tend to involve multiple different acts such as threats, intimidation, coercive control, possibly actual violence and sometimes homicide.

This means that there are multiple opportunities to develop traumatic memories. As explained in Chapter 6, these memories are so much more volatile, vivid and distressing than memories for non-traumatic events. These memories can also serve as a very effective reminder to a child of just how dangerous the world is, and how dangerous relationships can be. With domestic abuse, sometimes children do not see the actual violence, but they may hear the threats, arguments or fights and then imagine what is actually happening. Their imagination might be worse than the reality. The image they construct in their minds could then behave in much the same way as a memory for something that they actually witnessed.

These experiences accumulate and can have a devastating impact on children. If there are threats and violence at home – the very place where you are *supposed* to be safe, then it is easy to understand how children can struggle to see anywhere as safe. And if the threats and violence are perpetrated by someone who is *supposed* to care about them, or perhaps between two people that are *supposed* to love each other, then it is easy to see how children can struggle to trust anyone to keep them safe and have no faith in any relationship being positive. If a child's parents or carers are unable to love and protect the child consistently, then it is easy to see how a child can start to believe that they themselves must be unlovable.

For the child, the take-away message of the abuse may be that anywhere and anyone could be dangerous. This can lead to feelings of fear and lack of trust which are present all of the time. This makes it really difficult to manage life in the world, and particularly hard to develop healthy relationships and friendships. Children who have been abused are likely to find it particularly difficult to trust other adults who are trying to care for them because of the way their experiences have coloured their view of others and shaped their expectations of how others will treat them. They might feel safer if they can keep such adults at a distance, rather than have to rely on them. To achieve this, they could try to drive others away from them by being hostile and aggressive. This can make it quite hard to care for a child who has been abused.

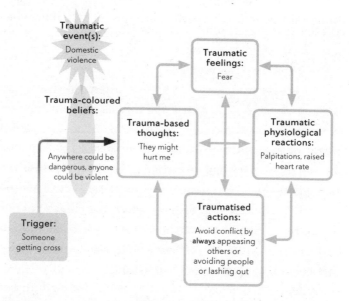

Seeing adults as potential threats and being hypervigilant to people showing emotions like anger may be a really useful safety strategy when a child is living in a home where violence is commonplace, but it might be difficult to change that tactic in other places, or when the violence has ended. In fact, that very strategy that previously kept the child safer could become problematic if it causes them to get into trouble at school, or if it prevents them from developing trusting relationships.

Children absorb the examples around them without even realising. If they are repeatedly exposed to examples of differences of opinion being settled by threats and violence, it is more likely they will resort to such strategies when they experience conflict with peers.

Abuse also seems to be particularly prone to making children feel guilty. Children might think that they caused the arguments between their parents, or that they should have stepped in to protect one adult from another. Sometimes the person responsible for the abuse will explicitly tell the child that it is their fault.

Domestic abuse and violence at home does not just change the way that the young person sees the world, themselves and others; it does not just provide them with multiple potentially traumatic memories to intrude into their consciousness in a vivid and distressing manner. It can actually change the way that their brain works. Professor McCrory and colleagues found that when looking at pictures of angry faces, two areas of the brain associated with threat perception (the anterior insula and the amygdala on the right side), were activated more than in the children who had not experienced violence in the home.[41] Children's brains have an amazing capacity to adapt to their environment, and this ability to notice potential threat and react to it so quickly may be incredibly helpful when living in the threatening situation. But it may not be so helpful outside of that threatening situation. In fact, seeing threat everywhere and reacting strongly and automatically to it can be extremely unhelpful in other situations. For example, how can a student learn if they are constantly scanning the environment for threats, or if when an adult teacher raises their voice the child assumes that they are about to be violent? There is lots of information about how a child's brain adapts to these sorts of situations, including a short helpful animation on the UK Trauma Council's website, details of which can be found in Appendix Three.

If your child is operating at a higher level of physiological arousal because of their past experiences, they could be prone to losing their temper more easily, more often and more severely. This in turn might be affecting their relationships. They might find it difficult to make or keep good friendships because they lose their temper. And that might mean they are missing out on the very social support that would help them to recover from their past.

Thinking about the Five Principles, it is crucial to ensure that they actually are safe enough. And that might involve taking them from the dangerous environment to stay somewhere safer. Then, once they are safe, helping them to *feel* safe and learn skills that enable them to calm down can be useful. But you and other adults around them, for example at school, might need to be a bit more proactive and provide some 'scaffolding' to help them with their friendships until things are a bit more well established, this can help with the feeling connected and social support. That scaffolding might be taking an active role in arranging visits to or from friends, it might mean that you are more aware of how long your child can manage before losing it, and so you keep visits shorter. But in order to draw on the principle of helping them to feel in control, you need to ensure that you are helping them to do things for themselves, and not taking their control away.

You can help them by being extremely patient, consistent and gentle. Don't expect a few positive experiences of a caring relationship to undo the damage straight away. As I explained in Chapter 7, a child's traumatic experiences can colour the way that they see things even when the trauma is over. So your child could see your attempts to love and nurture them through their particular lens. Regardless of how benevolent your actions actually are, they may expect you to behave just as others who were supposed to care for them did.

Because they have previously adapted to survive in an abusive environment, your child might be on the lookout for abusive experiences which means that they can see the potential for abuse where it doesn't actually exist. For example, many children can tolerate a parent or carer being ten minutes late to collect them; they might be a bit upset, but they will most likely respond to the reassurance offered while they are waiting, and will be relieved when their parent or carer arrives. But a child who has been emotionally abused might see the lateness as proof that their parent or carer does not love them. Similarly, many children can tolerate an adult getting cross with them. But when a child who has been physically abused, or who has witnessed domestic violence, sees the adult that is caring for them getting cross, they may have an extreme reaction, because their experience has taught them that angry adults can be violent and abusive.

But over time, if you can continue to provide consistent, patient, calm, loving care, you can start to provide over-whelming evidence that their world is benevolent, that carers can be safe and loving and that they are actually lovable. This might not be enough to 'recalibrate' their beliefs and the way that their brains work. You might need to work hard to help them realise that they are actually safe – this will involve a mixture of actions and words. You may need to have conversations with them and help them to recognise how their previous experiences might be colouring the way they see things, with a view to help-ing them to re-evaluate and rebalance their beliefs behind their feelings and actions. Rather than simply telling them your view (e.g. that it's not their fault), by being accepting and curious you can help them to reconsider things. For example, you might ask them questions about what would have happened if they had got more involved, or what they would say to a friend who was feeling guilty for something that an adult in their house did.

But be careful of 'challenging' their thoughts and beliefs too firmly, though – you may find that they close down and don't share their thinking with you. It can be helpful to be really validating and understanding. For example:

'To me, it makes complete sense that your brain sees the world like that. Look at what your stepdad used to do! I think most people would worry about whether or not they are safe. In fact, worrying about that was pretty useful before – it would have helped you to look out for those times that he was really angry and dangerous. Those times were so scary it's probably difficult for your brain to 'catch up' and realise that you're safe now. It got so used to living with danger that it can't get used to the fact that we're all safe now. Do you remember when we rearranged all of your toys and it took you a while to get used to the fact that your pens were in a different box and you kept looking in the old box for them? Well, keeping safe is so much more important than where your pens are, it makes sense that your brain would hold on to the old ideas – just in case. But you're safe now because . . .'

Sexual abuse

Sexual abuse is a very broad term that can cover a wide range of events where an adult (or young person) forces, tricks or entices a child into some form of sexual activity. Even without any sexual abuse, a child's early sexual activity and sexual development can be complicated enough, so it is no surprise that sexual abuse can be traumatic in some very complicated ways. It is difficult to get reliable statistics, but in 2019, the Crime Survey for England and Wales (CSEW) estimated that 7.5 per cent of adults had experienced sexual abuse before the age of sixteen.[42] In the US, it is estimated that around 25 per cent of 17 year olds have experienced sexual abuse or assault.[43]

Children might feel embarrassed or ashamed about what has happened, and could worry that others will judge them if they find out. This can make it very hard to tell anyone about what has happened. As a result, a great deal of sexual abuse goes unreported at the time. The perpetrator might have deliberately tried to prevent the child from disclosing the abuse by threatening violence, for example, or they may have told the child that if they tell anyone they will be removed from their family home. The perpetrator might tell the child that what has happened is their fault and that they will be in trouble if anyone finds out, or that no one will believe them if they tell them. Children who find it impossible to disclose abuse, or whose allegations are not believed, might end up having to cope with the abuse and its impact all on their own. They might feel isolated and believe that no one could possibly understand what has happened to them. The abuse might have been perpetrated by someone with whom the child had, or even has, a positive relationship in other ways, which can leave the child with some very complicated and confusing feelings towards the person.

As described throughout this book, the meaning that a child attributes to the potentially traumatic events is central to just how traumatic those events will actually be for them. The abuse might change the way they see themselves or the way they see others. They could, for example, begin to believe that they are worthless, only good for one thing, or damaged. These negative beliefs about themselves might lead them to avoid relationships completely and isolate themselves from their peers and family.

After sexual abuse, the child's normal sexual exploration, even within the context of a loving relationship, might trigger vivid, distressing, intrusive memories of the abuse, which could make the development of healthy sexual relationships very difficult. They might see themselves as damaged or even soiled in some way, and therefore find it difficult to have fulfilling relationships as adults. The abuse may leave them with the belief that people who ought to be able to care for them cannot be trusted to do so appropriately. This might lead them to become prematurely independent, or to rely on others inappropriately, which could then make them vulnerable to further abuse or exploitation.

If the child is able to disclose the abuse, or if it is discovered, what happens subsequently can make a significant difference to how the abuse impacts the child. If the child is not believed, this can add to their feelings of worthlessness and isolation. If the abuse is not investigated or if the perpetrator is not successfully prosecuted, then the child could feel that the world is a very unsafe place. In some situations, if the child remains living with the perpetrator, even if the abuse stops, they continue to feel vulnerable and unsettled.

All of this means that sexual abuse may be a particularly difficult trauma to help your child recover from. The intimate nature of the abuse could lead to overwhelming feelings of shame which might make it especially difficult to think about or talk about. And if your child is unable to think or talk about what happened, their thoughts, feelings and any difficulties they have, it's going to be more challenging for you to help with their recovery. Some ideas that might help include:

- If you are able to make the events 'talkable about', then that can be really helpful, but it may not be possible. Some children find it easier to talk to someone outside of their family, and this might be particularly true in relation to sexual abuse because of embarrassment and shame.

- If they are not able to talk about it with you, you might be able to help by talking *around* the sexual abuse without having to actually mention it directly. You could talk about common reactions (see Part 1) and check in with your child to see if any of these are familiar.

- You could talk about the 'quality' of memories without necessarily discussing the 'content'. You could help them to realise that memories for difficult, frightening or overwhelming events are sometimes different to memories for other events. The metaphors and cartoons described in Part 2 might help. This might not help your child to talk about what happened, but it might normalise their reactions, so they don't feel so weird for having nightmares or flashbacks.

- You could explain that sometimes after events like that, people start to see things differently; they might feel more vulnerable, perhaps feel they cannot trust people, and that the world is not safe. Then you could ask them if they feel any of those things since what happened. So, the abuse might be too difficult to talk about, but they might be able to talk about how they think and feel now.

One boy told me that he could cope with the abuse, it was the nightmares and flashbacks that he couldn't cope with because they made him think that he was going mad. He said that not only had the abuser messed with his body, he had also messed with his head, but it was the problems in his head that lasted. Finding a way to think through what happened and to put those fragmented images, sensations, thoughts and feelings into a coherent narrative can really help with children's flashbacks and nightmares. But because they are often so embarrassed or ashamed this can be particularly challenging. Some children find it easier to do this with the help of someone they do not have to see at other times, such as a therapist or counsellor. Whereas other children find it easier to do this with someone they know rather than a complete stranger. There are ideas for getting additional support in Appendix Three.

Key points

- Complex trauma refers to traumatic events that are repeated or persistent, and that are caused by someone else.

- The repeated or persistent nature of these events, together with the fact that they are caused by someone, tend to make the reactions more severe and more complicated.

- In supporting recovery from complex trauma, it will be helpful to consider how you could understand your child's experience of that trauma using the approaches outlined earlier in this book, and how you could apply the Five Principles.

- Children who have experienced complex trauma may find it particularly difficult to trust other people.

21

Health-related Trauma – Physical Injury and Illness

The 2017 survey of Mental Health of Children and Young People in England found that around 14 per cent of seventeen to nineteen year olds had been ill enough to have to spend a night in hospital, and that about 6 per cent had been involved, or badly hurt, in a serious accident .[44]

Injuries and illnesses often involve pain. Interestingly the same part of the brain (the amygdala) is central to both physical pain and fear. So, it is no surprise that memories of events that involve physical pain can be similar to other traumatic memories. Even if not painful and even if not *in reality* life-threatening, children might find an injury or illness frightening and therefore the associated memories may cause difficulty. Those memories often come to mind uninvited and can be very vivid. The physical pain of the original event is sometimes re-experienced. One girl told me that when she remembered what happened, the scar on her leg from the wound she received started to hurt again. She told me, 'It's as if the nerves in my leg can remember what happened and are reminding my brain of it.'

In addition to the pain involved, injuries and illness might challenge children's assumptions that they are safe and well. This can then colour the way that they perceive everyday things. For example, if a child has had a brain tumour which has been successfully removed with little lasting impact expected, it is wholly understandable that they might have a different response to a headache. They may well wonder if the tumour has returned. They might start to notice every twinge and sensation in their body and wonder if they are signs of cancer. Because the triggers are 'internal', those caring for them may not even be aware that the child is noticing and worrying about them.

Injury and illness might result in repeated hospital visits, which themselves have potential to be traumatic. Painful medical procedures may be necessary. But even if they are not subjectively especially painful, they might be perceived as being extremely frightening by children. Children could be so afraid of having an injection or of having blood taken that they get extremely distressed. Depending on how vital the procedure is, they might be forced to comply, which can be understandably upsetting, and emphasises how little control they have over what happens to them. If they subsequently need to attend hospital again, vivid distressing memories of the previous events could be triggered, so they may get very distressed again, and try hard to avoid hospital visits and medical procedures. Which may result in them being forced again. Health professionals might view this as 'procedural anxiety', but if the anxiety is 'fuelled' by past memories of previous procedures in a traumatic way, it might be necessary to help the child to process those memories before they are able to reduce their anxiety.

In hospitals or clinics, children may witness others who are very distressed or very ill. They may even be aware of the death of a fellow patient. The machines and medical paraphernalia might be extremely frightening to children who are unable to understand what they do and how. In certain circumstances, in order to avoid spreading infection, professionals may have to wear outfits that protect them from viruses. This might be terrifying to children who could see such precautions as having particularly negative meaning and they might over-estimate the actual risks.

Preparing children for medical procedures can be complicated – even just choosing the timing can be complex. If you tell them too far in advance they might have too much time to dwell on it and make it into something far bigger than it is. But if you spring it on them, they could feel that they have little control over things and might find it difficult to trust you. However, you know your child better than probably anyone else, so you hold crucial information about them and about how and when to tell them. It might be useful to discuss this with some other adults that know them well, not so that they can tell you what to do but so that you can check your ideas out with someone else. Repeated trips to hospitals for check-ups or further treatments might be very triggering, but could also provide opportunities to process previous traumatic experiences if you can help them to think through what happened in a calm enough state.

Simply explaining what is going to happen, explaining some of the unfamiliar machines around them and discussing what strategies they can use to cope can have a very beneficial impact. In UK hospitals, play specialists and paediatric psychologists are especially good at supporting children. So if these professionals have not been mentioned to you, it might be worth asking if they are available.

Key points

- Physical injury, illness and medical treatment have the potential to be traumatic.

- How frightened and how at risk a child feels is a better predictor of difficulties than the objective reality.

- Visits to a hospital or clinic may trigger memories of previous difficult visits.

- Well-timed, honest conversations and explanations can help decrease your child's anxiety.

22

Shared trauma – Traumatic events that Affect Groups of People

Some events are not experienced or witnessed by one or two people, but the experience is shared by many. In some ways, these events are different to the individual events described so far. It might be difficult to see the event as extraordinary if lots of people were involved. For that particular group of children, that event may be the norm – which can have positive and negative effects. It might be that children see others around them struggling and possibly having quite considerable reactions. And this might make them feel that they ought to be responding like that, or they may feel isolated if they do not respond in the same way as others. In Part 1, I described some of the very many different ways that children may react to traumatic events, so there really is no particular way that children tend to, or ought to, react to traumatic events.

Sometimes, talking with other people who have been through the same event can be extremely useful – some children feel better understood by someone who has been through the same thing or something similar. They might feel that they can only talk about their experiences with other people who have had the same or similar experiences, and when they do share their stories, they begin to change the quality of the memories (as described earlier in Part 2). They might also be able to share details that change their understanding of what happened as information is shared.

Children might feel very isolated with their reactions and worry that their distress and difficulties mean that there is something 'wrong' with them, or that they are permanently damaged. It can therefore be very reassuring to realise that other children are reacting in similar ways.

Pandemics

During pandemics, such as COVID-19 which swept around the world from 2020, in addition to the direct impact of the illness, there may also be additional psychological impact on children and young people as a result of measures taken to try to contain pandemics, such as lockdowns and social distancing.

Pandemics can lead to an increased number of deaths. This means that more children will be bereaved as a result. The deaths might have been sudden and unexpected, and due to measures taken to contain the disease, there might have been no opportunity to say goodbye to loved ones. If the health services were stretched at the time the person died, children and young people could believe that doctors had to choose whether to save their loved one or someone else. Following the death, it might not have been possible to view the body (which often helps children and young people to accept the death and provide an opportunity to say goodbye). Furthermore, funerals where large numbers of people gather together to say goodbye collectively and support each other through shared grief may not have been possible, or only possible for very limited numbers. There might have been a very clear public health message about the steps that can be taken to reduce the spread of the disease (such as social distancing and hand hygiene). This might mean that if someone dies, a child could worry that it was their fault for not washing their hands well enough. All of these make for a potent cocktail which increases the chances that children will find it more difficult to grieve and adjust to their loss.

Aside from the increased number and the increased complexity of bereavements, pandemics (and associated measures such as social distancing and lockdowns where households are less able to leave their homes) may increase the number of potentially traumatic events to which children are exposed.

Families being under increased stress, with fewer outlets and opportunities to feel supported, could lead to more strained relationships, some of which may lead to violence. During the 2020 lockdown in the UK, Refuge (UK's largest provider of domestic abuse support) received many more calls to its helpline. Then, as the restrictions eased, it experienced an increase in the number of women and children needing emergency accommodation. Households being stuck together and more isolated might increase the risk of abuse, and the children will have fewer opportunities to disclose anything that has happened to them. During lockdowns, those children who are already at risk may have fewer visits from professionals and less contact with trusted teachers – which again adds to the risk of them experiencing traumatic events.

Regardless of actual events that might happen to children during pandemics, they are likely to be exposed to repeated information from news media and social media about the dangers of the disease. Such accounts might not be balanced and may emphasise the risks. Children might not have the cognitive ability to be able to fully understand or challenge such reports, or to put them into perspective. Therefore, this exposure to information may colour their beliefs and distort their thinking.

With news media and social media so readily available, during pandemics, it is particularly important to manage the information to which your child has access. This is discussed in a previous section. They might also need support to process the trauma of the death so that they can start to grieve their loss, as discussed in an earlier section.

Terrorism

Terrorism involves violence and intimidation for political aims. Acts of terrorism often involve large numbers of people, usually civilians as opposed to military forces. The frequency and severity of terrorist acts tends to fluctuate from year to year, which makes it difficult to be sure whether it is increasing or not. But there is no doubt that children's potential to be made aware of it has increased significantly due to the internet, social media and news media.

The extent to which children will be traumatised by terrorist acts depends partly on the severity of the event and their exposure it. There is likely to be a difference between hearing about a bomb in another country which did not harm anyone, as opposed to being directly caught up in a terrorist attack which results in multiple casualties. However, more important than what children actually experience is what they make of it. This comes back to the earlier ideas of memory and meaning.

Following a terrorist act, some children might continue to believe that such events are rare and usually happen elsewhere, they will likely retain their assumptions that the world is generally not too risky and that they are safe enough. These children might have relatively mild reactions, even if they were directly involved. They may even think they were lucky that they survived.

Other children might not actually experience the event and only hear about it, but nonetheless, it could change their assumptions about how common such events are and how safe they are. This can lead them to feel that the world is too dangerous and that they are too vulnerable. These children might experience much more distress and difficulties.

Difficulties following terrorist acts are often associated with the understandable sense of fear that follows – that is exactly what many terrorists are trying to achieve. It therefore becomes important to help children develop a realistic evaluation of risk. This may not be very easy, because when a child (or in fact an adult) starts to feel afraid, they could find it difficult to think more reasonably, or they might try to avoid thinking it through because of the distress it causes. This avoidance make it very difficult to develop a balanced and realistic assessment of risk, but by picking your moments, and by using your knowledge of what helps your child to feel calm enough to be able to talk about their thoughts and feelings, you can start to help them to re-evaluate things. In fact, you might find that simply enabling them to get their fears out into the open, rather than locked away in their minds, starts to make a difference. Some fears simply disappear once they are talked through. Others might need a bit of coaxing and taming by you. But as mentioned elsewhere in this book, try to resist the temptation to tell your child that they are just being silly, and they've got nothing to fear. If you were to do that, there is a risk that they will stop sharing their fears with you and will be left to deal with them on their own.

Natural disasters and catastrophes

Each year, around the world, there are hundreds of natural disasters and catastrophes such as floods, storms, fires, earthquakes. These events can of course pose a very real and direct threat to a child's life and the lives of those around them. Deaths as a result of such events, may lead to traumatic memories or images, as I discussed earlier. In addition to any actual loss of life, these events may have far-reaching, real, negative consequences for children and families. For example, their home or even their neighbourhood might be damaged or destroyed, resulting in them having to move unexpectedly. They may not be able to take some of their loved, familiar or precious objects with them which can make children feel very unsafe and adds to the sense of loss. This upheaval can be very destabilising for children and families who are no longer able to retreat to the safety and familiarity of their home to make sense of events.

Such events are often widely reported in news and social media, and they are often commented upon by adults. So even if not directly affected by a disaster, a child's view of the world and how safe they are within it in can be significantly altered by disasters. They can make children believe that the natural world, rather than being benign and nurturing, is so unpredictable and dangerous that they may struggle to feel safe anywhere at any time. Some ideas that can help:

- In the immediate aftermath of a natural disaster it may be particularly difficult to provide for a child's basic needs such as safety, food, water and shelter. And these of course are the priority – both physically and psychologically. But even when things have settled, some children will continue to be anxious about such basic needs. I worked with one family where the children continued to be really anxious about meals; if their carers changed the time of a meal, or if it was a bit later than expected, they would get incredibly distressed. They could see that the food was on its way, but there seemed to be some very deep-rooted, almost unconscious, anxiety about whether they would be fed because of their past experience of going hungry.

- Some children can find small objects or toys very comforting. If it's possible for them to have an old familiar cuddly toy that can be 'rescued' then that can be extremely beneficial, but if that isn't possible then a new toy can soon become familiar and comforting.

- Following an event that destabilises the most basic of assumptions about the world being safe enough, ensuring that familiar routines and structure are in place, can be especially helpful.

- Explaining to children what is going to happen and when helps them to feel that at least some things in their lives are predictable. And this will help them to deal with the inevitable departures from the plan.

- You might want to have a week planner somewhere visible showing what is happening for the coming few days. You can then refer to it regularly so that your child remembers that the information is there. Although your child may rely on this to reassure them at first, as they start to feel more confident, they are likely to need it less and less, rather than become dependent upon it.

As mentioned elsewhere, you may want to spend some time exploring any fear and worries that your child has in case they have brought with them concerns that are based on their past experiences rather than their current situation.

War

In 2019, the charity Save the Children published a report which stated that nearly a fifth of the world's children are growing up in a conflict zone. The report goes on to point out that some military action takes no steps to reduce the impact on children, and some even intentionally targets children to deliberately induce terror. War usually involves multiple acts of severe, interpersonal, life-threatening violence – events that are highly likely to traumatise children. In addition to acts intended to kill and maim, war may also include capture and torture, involving pain and high levels of threat, which persist over a period of time. Of course such events are highly traumatic if experienced or witnessed by children.

Some children may feel guilty if someone is injured or killed trying to protect them. In some conflicts, children are actually coerced into becoming involved in the acts of war, which puts them at huge risk of extremely complicated trauma because of their active involvement in the traumatic events. In addition to the traumatic nature of the events, children and young people are frequently bereaved, with all of the additional difficulties that involves (mentioned elsewhere in this book). Some children will be aware that friends or family members have gone missing, but they might not know if they are still alive or not. This can be extremely distressing and complicated. Often children will hold on to hope that they are still alive, but that hope could be accompanied and engulfed by extreme distress as they then start to consider what the person might be going through. War may also directly affect a child's community, neighbourhood and home. Familiar places that ought to be a sanctuary are destroyed or are no longer considered safe.

It is easy to understand that war can be extremely traumatising for children. But the cognitive model described earlier in this book can be used to start to understand *how* those events become traumatic, by considering the role that memory, meaning and maintenance play. There are likely to be numerous, extremely violent and brutal, life-threatening events, any or all of which may form traumatic memories. As described earlier, even when the events are in the past and the child is in reality safe, these memories can keep the past events alive by vividly intruding into the child's waking and sleeping mind. The child might understandably find it hard to believe that they are safe because the acts of war have been so extreme and so pervasive, and have therefore 'infected' their view of themselves, the world and other people. Understandably, they might try hard NOT to think about the events because of the associated distress. This avoidance prevents them from processing the memories, putting them in the past and preventing them from developing a more realistic and useful view of their current situation.

Children who have experienced or witnessed war are particularly likely to suffer from the 'hyper-arousal' described earlier. They are likely to find it difficult to relax because they may be in a constant state of high alert. As such they could need additional help in managing triggers and their arousal levels. They could be very easily triggered by things that others might not even notice, such as police officers carrying weapons, or even just in uniform, toy guns, covering past wars in school lessons, news items about current wars, and dogs.

Some ideas that can help:

- Be aware of possible triggers and warn your child about anything they might come across that might trigger them.

- Let them know what to expect from day to day, so that they do not have to face uncertainty or surprises.

- Explain to them why their bodies are on such a high state of alert so much of the time and help them to develop strategies to calm themselves.

- Contacting the school so that they can be sensitive if they are going to be covering anything that may trigger a strong reaction.

But even with careful monitoring, comprehensive management of their expectations and pro-active contact with school, there are still very likely to be times that they are triggered (e.g. by a car back-firing, or a plane flying over). In such cases it will be useful to go through sections in this book that focus on strategies for managing arousal levels and helping them to calm.

Refugees and asylum seekers

Many refugees and asylum-seeking children will have experienced war, terrorism, or natural disasters and so it would be worth reading the previous sections on these to begin to understand how their experiences have affected them. However, other refugees and asylum seekers may be fleeing persecution that has not involved war but, by definition, will be fleeing something that is potentially traumatic, and their friends and family might have been directly caught up in whatever they are fleeing. In addition to the potentially traumatic events from which they are fleeing, there are a number of additional factors that add to the complexity of the situation for refugees and asylum seekers. They might have had extremely traumatic journeys from their home countries to the host country. The journey could have taken several years and included multiple dangerous events along the way. The journey might have involved periods of separation from their main carer, or they may have become permanently separated from their carers and had to fend for themselves or have been left in the 'care' of agents who have been paid to deliver the child to a certain country. They might not know if their family and friends are still alive, there might be no means of contacting them to find out, and even if there are, the child could worry that trying to contact their family might put them at increased risk or make them more vulnerable.

In the host country, in addition to trying to navigate a new country and culture, they might have very poor housing that does not feel safe, they might be moved frequently, they might be subject to racial abuse and attacks, they might feel isolated with no support, and they might struggle to learn a new language and therefore find it difficult to communicate their needs. They are likely to need interpreters at important appointments such as medical appointments or assessments of their needs, which can add significant difficulties. The same interpreter might not be available for each appointment, which can make it difficult to develop sufficient trust to be able to speak openly about their experiences, or their challenges. The child might not know the cultural background of the interpreter and therefore find it hard to trust them.

I have worked with some children who have experienced some dreadful events in their home country and have survived perilous journeys, but what they have found most distressing is their ongoing lack of safety in the host country. They had learned to expect their homes to be dangerous places, but had been led to believe that if they could make it to a host country such as the UK, they would be well cared for. Then when they arrive, they are not well cared for and as far as they are concerned, not only does the danger continue but they have also had their hopes and expectations shattered. They had developed a belief that certain places, such as their home country, were dangerous, but other places, such as the UK, would be safe. When this turns out not to be true, they develop the traumatic beliefs that nowhere is safe, that they are vulnerable and cannot trust anyone.

In some countries, the asylum-seeking process can drag on and on so that the children are in a constant state of anxiety, because until a decision has been made about their status, they are preoccupied with extreme worry that they will be returned to the danger from which they fled. This can make it difficult to help a child because they do not have an unrealistic sense of current threat based on past experiences, they have a sense of current threat based on a very real concern that they may be returned.

One of the most useful things that you can do for your child if they are going through the asylum-seeking process is try to help them navigate the legal process. And then help them to live with the uncertainly by partly acknowledging the difficulties and their concerns, but also helping them to balance that with what they do know and what they can rely upon.

If their first language is different to the language of the country in which they are living, it can be useful to focus on helping them to learn the local language, as well as finding others that speak their own language for them to connect to.

Key points

- Events that are experienced or witnessed by groups of people, such as terrorism, natural disasters, war and pandemics, can lead children to feel isolated if they do not respond in the same way as others.

- A child does not need to be directly involved in the event for it to have a significant impact.

- The approaches outlined throughout this book can help address the traumatic memories and meanings from events that affect groups of people.

PART V

<><><><><><><><><><>

It's All About You. Well, Not ALL About You, But Quite a Bit About You.

If you are reading this book, then you are probably keen to work out what is going on with your child, and how best to help them. That's great – and your child is lucky to have you investing time and effort in helping them. But what about you? If you really want to do what's best for your child, then it's important that you make sure that *you* are in good enough shape psychologically to be able to help them. You can't water plants with a leaky watering can! You need to look after your watering can enough so that it can water and feed your plants, which means that they will be able to grow and flourish. It is also possible that you have been directly affected by the same event or events that your child experienced. You might have had the same traumatic experience, or if your child is affected by a bereavement it is quite likely you have also lost some-one close to you. The reactions and difficulties your child is experiencing might be all too familiar to you and you might benefit from some care and attention to recover, both as a parent and as a person.

23

Why It Is Important for You to Take Care of Yourself and What to Look Out For

It's vital that as part of caring for your child, you stop for a moment to think about how *you* are doing and what would help *you* – so that you can best help your child. This is not an act of selfishness; it's simply ensuring that your child gets the best help possible so that they have the best chance of recovery.

I have worked with lots of loving and excellent parents and carers after traumatic events who try to downplay their own needs – they say things like, 'I just need to focus on the children, if they are OK, then I can be OK.' I try to help them understand that unless they, the carers, are OK, it's pretty unlikely that the children will have a chance of being OK. When you get on a plane, and are given the safety briefing, they always say in case of an emergency put *your* oxygen mask on before you try to help anyone else with *their* mask. Most people can see the logic of that – if we can't breathe then there's a limit to how much we can help others. It's the same principle here: looking after yourself enough will mean that you can best help your child.

In 2012, some colleagues and I reviewed research that had studied children and young people after various traumatic events. We evaluated the strength of the connection between lots of different risk factors and the child's symptoms of PTSD.[45] We found sixty-four studies, which in total had assessed more than 30,000 children following potentially traumatic events. By combining the results we were able to predict why some children developed PTSD and how severe their symptoms of PTSD were. We found that 'trauma severity' (i.e. an objective measure of how big or bad the traumatic event was) was exactly the same size risk factor as the carer's mental health. This means that the link between how big or bad the trauma was and how your child is doing, is the same size as the link between how you are doing and how your child is doing.

So, it is worth taking a few moments to stop and think about how you are doing. What might you need to help you support your child in the best possible way? If you were a professional therapist you would have regular supervision, when you could check in with your supervisor to think about how you are doing and how the work you do might affect you, and how able you are to support others. As a professional therapist you might also have access to an occupational counselling scheme, because organisations involved in mental health realise that to offer the best help they can to clients, it is important to look after the therapists. If you are the child's carer, then you are spending much *more* time with your child than any therapist and can't go home at the end of the day to switch off. So your needs might be even greater than a therapist's and looking after *you* is even more important.

Your wellbeing is important because you are central to your child's recovery

One of the problems with traumatic events and bereavements, is that they often increase anxiety in everyone concerned, not just those directly affected. I have worked with many parents who feel perfectly able to help their children with difficult or stressful experiences, but after potentially traumatic events or bereavements they suddenly feel unable to help their children because they do not have specialist training and knowledge.

As their carer, you have particular knowledge of, and insight into, your child. You probably know them better than anyone else. You get to see them at times that no one else does and you might have extensive knowledge of what they were like before the events or losses. This means that you can expertly understand their behaviour and what they are experiencing in ways that probably no one else can. This special knowledge, combined with your close relationship with them, and the time that you get to spend with them, means that you are *uniquely* positioned to help them after difficult or potentially traumatic events and losses. This book is hopefully helping you to understand trauma and loss better, and have a deeper understanding of what might help. This might also reduce your anxiety and give you the confidence to help them. Because when it comes to your child, you really are the expert, and you have a central role in helping them. Your relationship with them is a fundamental part of their psychological environment, and can play a crucial part in supporting their recovery. But if you are not in a good enough place yourself, then that will reduce how helpful your relationship with them can be.

If you're worried that you might get it wrong, or that you cannot cope, then you are probably on the right track as you are actively thinking about what would be most helpful and your concern about getting it wrong shows how important it is to you to help your child. You might want to consider getting some help or support for *you* – your friends, family, neighbours, school staff, etc., might all be able to offer some additional support, to help you to help your child.

Checking in with yourself

Just as I encouraged you to stop and think specifically about how your child is doing, it's worth doing the same for you.

What follows is not a formal questionnaire, there is no scoring system. It is just a list of areas for you to stop and think about. For each item, tick if it's been a problem for you over the last two weeks. And then, for the ticked items, ask yourself what would help it to be less of a problem.

There is another copy in Appendix One, and additional copies can be downloaded from https://overcoming.co.uk/715/resources-to-download.

Feeling sad a lot of the time	❏
Feeling pessimistic or hopeless about the future	❏
Having no confidence in yourself	❏
Getting little or no pleasure out of things that you used to enjoy	❏
Feeling restless lots of the time	❏
Not being interested in other people or things	❏
Having little or no energy	❏
Being easily irritated, snapping at people	❏
Eating a lot	❏
Eating little	❏
Having difficulties concentrating	❏
Feeling tired a lot of the time	❏
Having difficulties falling asleep or staying asleep	❏
Feeling worried or anxious a lot of the time	❏
Getting worried or panicky when you don't really need to	❏

Finding it difficult to relax	❏
Feeling unable to cope	❏
Having aches and pains without physical causes	❏
Feeling like crying a lot	❏
Having unwanted images or memories pop into your mind	❏
Having unhelpful thoughts going round and round in your head	❏
Having nightmares or bad dreams	❏
Re-experiencing a bad event repeatedly	❏
Trying hard not to think about something or remember something	❏
Avoiding places, things or people	❏
Feeling on the lookout when there is no need to	❏
Feeling very jumpy	❏
Not feeling connected to friends and family	❏
Feeling alone and isolated	❏
Finding it difficult to get on with other people	❏
Finding it difficult to make decisions	❏
Staying in more than usual	❏

There may be other difficulties that you think of while going through this list, feel free to add them.

If you identify any areas that seem like they might be getting in the way of you being able to provide the best recovery environment for your child, then it's worth thinking about what you can do. And if you don't identify any problems, it's worth thinking about how you can keep yourself in the best possible shape to prevent difficulties arising.

Key points

- You can play a fundamental role in establishing the environment for your child's recovery, and your relationship with your child can play a crucial part in supporting their recovery.

- But if you are struggling yourself, then that will reduce how helpful you can be.

- With this in mind, you might find it helpful to check in with yourself and work out ways that you can take care of yourself, so that you are aware of how you're doing.

24

How to Help Yourself

Basics

First, you need to make sure that you are taking care of *your* basic needs as much as possible, before you are able to really be most useful for your child:

- Are you eating well enough?

- Do you have a good enough bedtime routine to help you sleep?

- If you wake up in the night with your head spinning, do you have a notepad where you can jot down your thoughts and 'park' your anxieties?

- Are you turning off your devices at least one hour before bed?

- Are you taking some regular exercise or at least getting outside most days?

- Are you taking some time to stop and pause or is it all go-go-go?

- Are you writing things down, both to manage

anxiety and also to help plan and set goals? It can be easy to forget to do this, or to think you will remember or don't need to but the simple act of writing things down can be surprisingly helpful.

Sometimes when we are so busy trying to look after someone else, we don't quite get around to meeting our own basic needs, which then makes it harder to care for someone else.

Those Five Principles again

You may remember that much of the rest of this book has focused on five evidence-based principles for helping your child. Well, those same five principles can be applied to *you* and *your own* wellbeing.

How can YOU feel safe?

That might seem like an odd question – but think about safety in the broadest possible terms. Think about stability and security as well as physical safety. Is your financial situation secure enough? Is your housing situation stable enough? Are there any big changes coming up for you that might unsettle things for you? It may feel as if there is little that you can do about some of these, but if any of them are taking away from your sense of security, it would be worth stopping and thinking about what could be done.

In England, Scotland and Wales, the Citizen's Advice Bureau (contact details are in the Appendix Three) can often offer advice about some of these basic needs. And the CAB website also has links for some places that can help in Northern Ireland. There may be other sources of support or help from your local council or from charities. Outside of the UK there may be other services that can help with these fundamental and basic needs. You will be in a better place to help your child once you have done all that you can to ensure these basic needs are met.

How can YOU feel calm?

The first thing to do here, is to 'mind your mind'. What I mean by this is to observe what's going on in your mind – notice what you are thinking and what you are feeling. Usually, we are so busy doing things or attending to what everyone else is doing, thinking or feeling, that we often don't notice what we are thinking or feeling.

This can be especially difficult (and yet particularly important) when our children are having some sort of crisis. We may get very wrapped up in their situation such that we end up 'reacting' rather than responding. Sometimes, the trick is to briefly extract yourself, take a step back, take a breath, think about what's going on, notice how it's making you feel, and then return and respond. We're not talking about popping off for a sleep and a full reboot, we're talking about taking a breath and having a think. It might be useful to remind yourself of how trauma and loss affect your child and might have changed the way that they see things. That might explain some of their actions and reactions, which will help you to work out how best to respond. For example, if they are having a meltdown just as it's time to go to school it can be useful to try to work out if there is anything about their experiences which might be colouring the way that they see going to school. Are they worried what their friends will ask or say to them? Is there someone or something at school that will remind them of their trauma or their loss? Applying this detective approach to what is going on can help you to feel calm and more able to deal with the situation.

If you think that you are struggling to feel calm, it would be worth taking a look at the section of this book on how to help your child to feel calm – there may well be some strategies there that you could use too.

If it is worry that is stopping you from feeling calm, you might want to consider using what some people call a 'worry tree'. This is simply a structured way to decide what to do about your worries. It can help avoid getting sucked in a negative spiral where anxious thoughts, lead to more anxiety and worry. It can also help to make a plan on what action to take and how to move forward.

Worry Tree

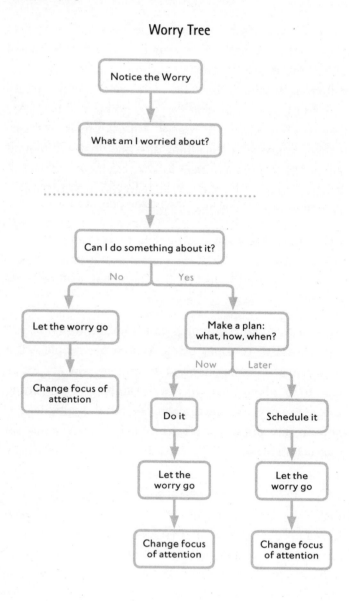

How can YOU feel connected?

When you are busy trying to do the best for your children, it's important to nurture your own support system. Sometimes parents and carers find it hard to make the time for this, or they might feel guilty investing in their own friendships. But sometimes, if people avoid spending time and connecting with others, it gets increasingly difficult to do so, and people get stuck in one of those unhelpful cycles of avoidance that I've described elsewhere. You're too busy to connect with others – relationships start to weaken – it's more difficult to connect.

Who are the partners, friends, family, colleagues, neighbours, etc., that form part of your web of healthy and positive connections? This is different to the team of people that might be involved with helping your child. This is about the people that *you* feel connected to and that will help *you* as you help your child. It's OK to have different people to perform different roles – you may have one who is great at offering you practical support, another that is great to talk to when you want to puzzle something out, someone else who is great at providing emotional support and another one who is just funny and makes you laugh. There are so many easy ways to stay connected to others that it doesn't have to be difficult. But it does sometimes take a little bit of time, and you might feel that you don't have time. I'm just talking about making sure you do what you need to do to ensure you stay connected to your network. You may want to connect with other parents and carers who are in a similar situation but be a little bit careful about whom you connect with, you want to make sure that your connections are healthy and good for you.

Relationships with partners can be affected by what happens to your child. You may find yourself spending less time communicating with them because your child takes priority. But this may be just the time that you could benefit more than ever from a close relationship, so you may want to consider ways that you can invest in those important relationships.

How can YOU feel in control

I've described in previous parts of the book how traumatic events can skew your child's view of the world, themselves and others, and how you can help them to develop more balanced and helpful views. Well, the same mechanism might be at play with you. The events that have happened, and your child's subsequent difficulties could have left you believing that you have no control over anything, so you may as well give up trying; or they might have left you feeling as if you have to control everything. These two extremes are not realistic, not balanced and may not be helpful.

Take a moment and think about how much you are in control of things. What things *can* you control? What things do you have no control over? And what things are in the middle – things that you can have some influence over, but only some?

Then the trick is to not fret about those things that you can't control and 'let them go' (using the Worry Tree approach mentioned above can help). Of course it's not quite as easy as that, but it helps to step out of your worry for a moment and realise that there are some things that you can't control. Then it's easier to make a choice about whether to worry about them or not. Focus on those things that you can control or influence and work out how best to influence them. Work out how much effort is going to be required, and what are the chances of success. And if that 'cost-benefit' doesn't add up, then, again, try to let it go. Athletes are particularly good at this, at least the successful ones are. They tend to be really good at identifying and focusing on the 'controllables'.

It's also helpful to remind yourself that although you might feel you have little or no control over some things, there are some everyday things that you can have quite a lot of control over. You might even want to 'reclaim' some of the control that you had before the loss or trauma. You could plan a trip or plan a meal. And if you were to do that together with your child, then you would both be reminding yourselves of some of the way that you can still have an influence over some things.

How can YOU feel hopeful

You might find yourself worrying too much about the past and what has already happened. Or you may be so caught up in the here and now that you have little time to think about the future and what would be a 'good outcome' for you. It can be helpful to stop and think about the future, and to think about what a positive future would be like for you and your child. You don't have to dream up the perfect scenario, but it might help to think about those little victories, or those little things that you can tick off your list as having achieved. This is not about pretending the trauma or the loss didn't happen, and it's not about trying to minimise it. It is just about holding onto some positive thoughts about the future, alongside all the other things that are going on.

For example you might want to pause for a short time and think about how you hope things will be in a year's time, or three years. What are your hopes for how your child will be doing, and what you will have achieved? You can weave into this thinking the strengths that you and your child have that will help you to get there.

This positive future thinking can provide some respite from other preoccupations and help you to approach other things more positively.

Reaching out for additional support for you

If you feel that you are not on top of things, and could do with a little additional support to get you through, in the UK your GP might be good place to start to find access to additional sources of support such as counselling or therapy if that is what is needed. If you live in England you can usually refer yourself directly to the local NHS talking therapies service. Information about how to do this and other support that might be helpful is included in the Resources section. I have also included some organisations and sources of support that are specifically for adults who have experienced bereavement or trauma.

Or there may be some simple things that you can do to make your life a bit easier. You may also find it useful to contact a voluntary organisation who could offer some additional support. There are plenty of self-help guides around that you might like to consider. Details of some organisations and resources are listed in Appendix Three.

Key points

- Your wellbeing is crucial to your child's recovery.

- How are you applying the Five Principles to yourself?

- Consider if you need to take any steps to feel safer, calmer, more connected to others, in control and hopeful.

- It might be of benefit to you and your child to reach out for support for yourself from others, including professionals.

Final Thoughts

Children are remarkably resilient. They have a sort of built-in self-righting mechanism that enables them to bounce back from all sorts of things that happen to them. But of course, sometimes things can happen that knock them off course and they need some additional support. In this book, I've tried to use the best research available to guide you as to what sort of support you can provide that will increase their chance of recovery. And although you can *influence* their recovery, you cannot *control* it. It is not *all* down to you. Feel free to take plenty of credit if your child recovers well. But some children will continue to struggle despite your best efforts and may need some specialist help and support – that is not your fault. Particularly after loss or trauma, parents and carers sometimes put themselves under immense pressure to be perfect, as if they feel the need to somehow make up for what has happened to their children. If you set yourself the goal of being perfect, I'm pretty sure that you are going to fall short of that (no offence). And that might make you feel bad, guilty, useless. And those feelings are not going to help you to look after your child. As you know, real life can be pretty messy, and we are all flawed. But if you've bothered to read this book about how to help your child, that says something significant about how amazing you are, and how lucky your child is to have you. Hang on in there.

Appendix 1: Blank Copies of Resources from Earlier in the Book

Here are copies of checklists and tables that have been mentioned in the book. More copies are available to download for free from https://overcoming.co.uk/715/resources-to-download.

Checklist of child's difficulties (Chapter 3)

1) Intrusive Memories

Having nightmares (including bad dreams which are not directly related to the event(s)) ❏

Re-experiencing sensations (images, smells, sounds, tastes, touches) related to the events ❏

Flashbacks – acting or feeling as if it is happening again ❏

Having thoughts about the events that intrude into their minds or keep going round and round ❏

Repeatedly playing out or drawing particular parts of the events, or themes related to them ❏

Suddenly or repeatedly talking about the traumatic events ❏

Experiencing intense reactions to reminders ❏

2) Avoidance

Trying not to talk about the events ❏

Trying to avoid people, activities or places that might remind them or make them think about the events ❏

Being reluctant to go to bed or sleep ❏

Keeping their minds busy with other things ❏

3) Physiological Arousal

Having difficulties in going to sleep or staying asleep ❏

Having night terrors (see description above) ❏

Sleepwalking ❏

Being irritable, losing temper easily, being angry or violent ❏

Being jumpy, or easily startled ❏

Freezing in response to perceived threats ❏

Being hypervigilant or having concentration problems ❏

Being overly sensitive to sensory stimulation ❏

4) Anxiety

Being reluctant to leave carers or clingy ❏

Having new fears ❏

Feeling panicky ❏

Losing confidence ❏

Feeling generally worried ❏

Having obsessions and compulsions; having to check that they have done certain things ❏

Suffering from headaches, tummy aches, or other physical symptoms ❏

Having a change in appetite ❏

5) Dissociation – Feeling numb and disconnected

Appearing spaced out or in a daze ☐

Forgetting things easily ☐

Not remembering what they were doing for periods of time ☐

Losing track of time ☐

Feeling detached from themselves (e.g. referring to themself as 'he' or 'she') ☐

Daydreaming ☐

Blanking out when stressed ☐

Feeling emotionally numb and disconnected (i.e. seeming flat or as if they don't have the normal range of emotions) ☐

6) Other changes in thoughts and feelings

Having inaccurate thoughts about consequences of the events ☐

Developing omen formations (i.e. thinking they knew it was going to happen) ☐

Feeling very sad, much of the time ☐

Finding it difficult to enjoy anything ☐

Feeling distant or cut-off from others ☐

Lacking motivation to do things, even things they used to enjoy ☐

Seeing everything in a very negative way ☐

Wanting to die ☐

7) Other reactions

Feeling guilty	❑
Regressing (i.e. losing some developmental skills that they had mastered)	❑
Parentification	❑
Amnesia – being unable to remember significant parts of the event	❑
Taking longer for emotions to pass	❑
Having problems at school	❑
Taking risks	❑
Deliberately hurting themselves	❑

TOTAL

Blank Formulation (Chapter 9)

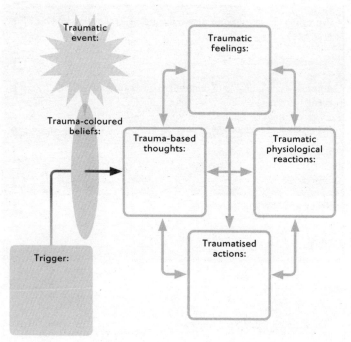

Before – During – After Table (Chapter 9)

Where and when	Before	During	After
	What was happening before?	What exactly did they do?	Who did what afterwards?
	What was the child doing?	(Describe behaviour, not thoughts and feelings.)	Was there any possible gain for the child?
	What were others doing?		
	Did anything seem to trigger them?		

Reviews
(Chapter 11 to Chapter 15)

Quick post-trauma review – SAFE

From 0 to 5, how does your child's environment (the things, the people, the places around them), and their own resources and abilities support a sense of safety?

_____

What helps?

_____

_____

_____

_____

_____

What ideas from the chapter that you have just read might you try to increase this further?

_____

_____

_____

_____

_____

Quick Post-trauma Review – Calm

From 0 to 5, how does your child's environment (the things, the people, the places) and their abilities support a sense of calmness?

_____

What helps?

_____

_____

_____

_____

_____

_____

What ideas from the section that you have just read might you try, to increase this further?

_____

_____

_____

_____

_____

_____

_____

Quick Post-trauma Review – Social Support and Connection

From 0 to 5, how does your child's environment (the things, the people, the places) and their abilities support a sense of social support and connections?

_____

What helps?

_____

_____

_____

_____

_____

_____

What ideas from the section that you have just read might you try, to increase this further?

_____

_____

_____

_____

_____

_____

Quick Post-trauma Review – In Control

From 0 to 5, how does your child's environment (the things, the people, the places) and their abilities support a sense of feeling in control?

_____

What helps?

_____

_____

_____

_____

_____

_____

What ideas from the section that you have just read might you try, to increase this further?

_____

_____

_____

_____

_____

_____

_____

Quick Post-trauma Review – Hopefulness

From 0 to 5, how does your child's environment (the things, the people, the places) and their abilities support a sense of hopefulness?

_____

What helps?

_____

_____

_____

_____

_____

_____

What ideas from the section that you have just read might you try, to increase this further?

_____

_____

_____

_____

_____

_____

_____

Checking in with yourself checklist (Chapter 23)

For each item, tick if it's been a problem for you over the last two weeks. And then, for the ticked items, ask yourself what would help it to be less of a problem.

Feeling sad a lot of the time	❑
Feeling pessimistic or hopeless about the future	❑
Having no confidence in yourself	❑
Getting little or no pleasure out of things that you used to enjoy	❑
Feeling restless lots of the time	❑
Not being interested in other people or things	❑
Having little or no energy	❑
Being easily irritated, snapping at people	❑
Eating a lot	❑
Eating little	❑
Having difficulties concentrating	❑
Feeling tired a lot of the time	❑
Having difficulties falling asleep or staying asleep	❑
Feeling worried or anxious a lot of the time	❑

Getting worried or panicky when you don't really need to	❏
Finding it difficult to relax	❏
Feeling unable to cope	❏
Having aches and pains without physical causes	❏
Feeling like crying a lot	❏
Having unwanted images or memories pop into your mind	❏
Having unhelpful thoughts going round and round in your head	❏
Having nightmares or bad dreams	❏
Re-experiencing a bad event repeatedly	❏
Trying hard not to think about something or remember something	❏
Avoiding places, things or people	❏
Feeling on the lookout when there is no need to	❏
Feeling very jumpy	❏
Not feeling connected to friends and family	❏
Feeling alone and isolated	❏
Finding it difficult to get on with other people	❏
Finding it difficult to make decisions	❏
Staying in more than usual	❏

Appendix 2: Relaxation Scripts

Below are three relaxation scripts that you might like to try with your child. I'd suggest asking your child to get comfortable in a quiet place (either lying down or sitting) at a time when you will not be interrupted. You can then read these out exactly as they are written if you wish, but they are really just to give you some ideas; you don't have to stick to these particular words. The more you ad lib, the more you can adapt the words to your particular child and find things that work for them, and the more it will be natural.

Some of the scripts use particular imagery to help engage the child in a playful way; of course if any of those images are going to trigger something about the trauma then change them. Or if you have ideas that are more meaningful to your child, use those instead.

Don't forget to use your tone of voice and your speed of speech to add to the feeling of relaxation.

If your child is particularly self-conscious about their body, they may find it upsetting to focus so much on it, in which case change the focus to the feeling of relaxation rather than parts of their body. Or use the Special Space script below.

In Chapter 6, I explained how memories for traumatic events have a tendency to intrude into children's minds. If you leave too many gaps when doing these relaxation scripts, you might find that memories from the trauma will fill the gaps. So without making it unrelaxing, you might find it better to be quite 'active' in the relaxation and make sure that your child has plenty to be thinking about so that the traumatic memories don't have space to spoil things.

It can be really helpful to get feedback from your child after giving these sorts of exercises a try. Were there any bits that they found particularly useful? Were there any bits that didn't really work? What changes do they suggest?

If your child found these helpful you might want to record these for them so can listen whenever they want.

Body relaxation script for children including imagery

Based on Koeppen, A. S. (1974). Relaxation training for children. *Elementary School Guidance & Counseling*, 9(1), 14-21; and Ollendick, T. H., & Cerny, J. A. (2013). *Clinical behavior therapy with children*. Springer Science & Business Media.

Introduction

So, we're going to practice some special kinds of exercises called relaxation exercises. These can help you to learn how to relax when you're feeling up-tight and help you get rid of those butter-flies-in-your-stomach kinds of feelings. They're also kind of cool because you can learn how to do some of them without anyone really noticing.

If you want to get the best out of these exercises, it's best to listen carefully to the instructions and do your best to follow them – even if they seem kind of silly. And all the way through, try hard to pay attention to your body and your muscles – focus on how your muscles feel when they are tight and how they feel different when they are loose and relaxed. If anything starts to hurt, then of course stop doing what you are doing and let me know.

Finally, don't forget, the more you practice the better you'll get at relaxing.

Any questions?

Are you ready to begin? Okay, first, get as comfortable as you can in your chair. Move around a bit if you want so that you get comfortable. Sit back, get both feet on the floor, and just let your arms hang loose. [Adjust this to fit with wherever your child is when doing the exercise]. *That's fine. Now, if you are OK to do it, close your eyes. While we are doing this exercise, it doesn't matter if you need to move a little bit just to make yourself more comfortable, you don't have to sit absolutely still during this. Here we go.*

Hands and Arms

Pretend you have a whole lemon in one of your hands. Now squeeze it hard. Try to squeeze all the juice out. Feel the tightness in your hand and arm as you squeeze.

Now drop the lemon. Notice how your muscles feel when they are relaxed.

Take another lemon in the same hand and squeeze. Try to squeeze this one harder than you did the first one. That's right. Really hard.

Now, drop the lemon and relax. See how much better your hand and arm feel when they are relaxed.

Once again, take a lemon in the same hand and squeeze all the juice out. Don't leave a single drop. Squeeze hard. Good.

Now relax and let the lemon fall from your hand.

And now, let's try the other hand. (Repeat the process for the other hand and arm.)

Arms and Shoulders

Pretend you are a furry, lazy cat. You want to stretch. Stretch your arms out in front of you. Raise them up high over your head. Way back. Feel the pull in your shoulders. Stretch higher.

Now just let your arms drop back to your side.

Okay, let's stretch again. Stretch your arms out in front of you. Raise them over your head. Pull them back, way back. Pull hard.

Now let them drop again. Good. Notice how your shoulders feel more relaxed. This time let's have a great big stretch. Try to touch the ceiling. Stretch your arms way out in front of you. Raise them way up high over your head. Push them way, way back. Notice the tension and pull, in your arms and shoulders. Hold tight, now. Great.

Let them drop and feel how good it is to be relaxed. It feels good, and loose, and warm.

Jaw

You have a thick jelly sweet in your mouth. It's hard to chew. Bite down on it. Hard! Let your neck muscles help you.

Now relax. Just let your jaw hang loose. Notice how good it feels just to let your jaw drop.

Okay, let's tackle that sweet again now. Bite down. Hard! Try to squeeze it out between your teeth. That's good. You're really tearing that sweet up.

Now relax again. Just let your jaw drop off your face. It feels good just to let go and not have to fight that sweet.

Okay, one more time. We're really going to tear it up this time. Bite down. Hard as you can. Harder. Oh, you're really working hard. Good.

Now relax. Try to relax your whole body. You've beaten that sweet. Let yourself go as loose as you can.

Face and Nose

Here comes a pesky old fly. He has landed on your nose. Try to get him off without using your hands. That's right, wrinkle up your nose. Make as many wrinkles in your nose as you can. Scrunch your nose up really hard. Good.

You've chased him away. Now you can relax your nose.

Oops, here he comes back again. Right back in the middle of your nose. Wrinkle up your nose again. Shoo him off. Wrinkle it up hard. Hold it just as tight as you can. Notice that when you scrunch up your nose your cheeks and your mouth and your forehead and your eyes all help you, and they get tight too.

Okay, he flew away. Relax your nose, and notice how your whole body relaxes too, and that feels good.

Oh-oh. This time that old fly has come back, but this time he's on your forehead. Make lots of wrinkles. Try to catch him between all those wrinkles. Hold it tight now.

Okay, you can let go. He's gone for good. Now you can just relax. Let your face go smooth, no wrinkles anywhere. Your face feels nice and smooth and relaxed.

Stomach

Hey! Here comes a cute baby elephant. But he's not watching where he's going. He doesn't see you lying in the grass, and he's about to step on your stomach. Don't move. You don't have time to get out of the way. Just get ready for him. Make your stomach very hard. Tighten up your stomach muscles really tight. Hold it.

You can relax now. It looks like he is going the other way. Let your stomach go soft. Let it be as relaxed as you can. That feels so much better.

Oops, he's coming this way again. Get ready. Tighten up your stomach. Really hard. If he steps on you when your stomach is hard, it won't hurt. Make your stomach as hard as a rock.

Okay, he's moving away again. You can relax now. Kind of settle down, get comfortable, and relax. Notice the difference between a tight stomach and a relaxed one. That's how we want to feel — nice and loose and relaxed.

You won't believe this, but this time he's coming your way and no turning around. He's headed straight for you. Tighten up. Tighten hard. Here he comes. This is really it. You've got to hold on tight. He's stepping on you.

He's stepped over you. Now he's gone for good. You can relax completely. You're safe. Everything is okay, and you can feel nice and relaxed.

This time imagine that you want to squeeze through a narrow fence and the boards have splinters on them. You'll have to make yourself narrow as possible if you're going to make it through. Suck your stomach in. Try to squeeze it up against your backbone. Try to be narrow as you can. You've got to be as thin as possible now.

And now just relax and feel your stomach being warm and loose.

Okay, let's try to get through that fence again. Squeeze up your stomach. Make it touch your backbone. Get it really small and tight. Get it as skinny as you can. Hold tight, now. You've got to squeeze through.

You can relax now. You got through that narrow little fence and no splinters! Settle back and let your stomach come back out where it belongs. You can feel really good now. You've done well.

Legs and Feet

Now pretend that you are standing barefoot in a big, muddy puddle. Squish your toes down deep into the mud. Try to get your feet down to the bottom of the mud puddle. You'll probably need your legs to help you push. Push down, feel the mud squish up between your toes.

Now step out of the mud puddle. Relax your feet. Let your toes go loose, give them a wiggle if you want, and feel how nice that it feels to be relaxed.

Back into the mud puddle. Squish your toes down. Let your leg muscles help push your feet down. Push your feet. Hard. Try to squeeze that puddle dry.

Okay. Come back out now. Relax your feet, relax your legs, relax your toes. It feels so good to be relaxed. No tight feelings anywhere. You feel kind of warm and tingly.

Closing

Stay as relaxed as you can. Let your whole body go limp and feel all your muscles relaxed. In a few minutes I will ask you to open your eyes, and that will be the end of this practice session.

As you go through the day, remember how good it feels to be relaxed. Sometimes you have to make yourself tighter before you can be relaxed, just as we did in these exercises. The more that you practice these exercises the better you'll get at relaxing and the quicker you'll be able to do it. A good time to practice is at night, after you have gone to bed and the lights are out and you won't be disturbed. It will help you get to sleep. Then, when you are really a good relaxer, you can help yourself relax at school or anywhere. Just remember the elephant, or the sweet, or the mud puddle, and you can do our exercises and nobody will know. Today is a good day, and you feel very relaxed, and ready for whatever is next. You've worked hard and it feels good to work hard. Very slowly, now, open your eyes and wiggle your muscles around a little. Very good. You've done a good job. You're going to be a champion relaxer.

Basic relaxation script

So, make yourself comfortable, you might need to just shuffle around or something. Remember while we are doing this exercise, it doesn't matter if you need to move a little bit just to make yourself more comfortable, you don't have to sit absolutely still during this. Then, when you are comfortable, if you are happy doing so then close your eyes, you'll find this makes it easier to concentrate on the feelings inside your body, but if you're not happy closing your eyes, that's fine as well.

Then, first of all just become aware of the noises around us, maybe you can hear people in the corridor, or maybe there are noises outside the window, or maybe there are some noises in the room that you can hear. [Adapt this to make it relevant to the environment you and your child are in]. *Turn your attention to those noises. And then gradually draw your attention in so that you're paying attention to things that are going on inside your own body rather than outside.*

The first thing I'd like you to pay attention to is your breathing. I don't want you to do anything to it, just notice the way that you breathe, the way that you breathe in . . . and breathe out. [Try to match the timing here to your child's actual breathing] *Feel the air going in through your nose and mouth, down your throat and filling your lungs. And then going out. As you're noticing your breathing, you'll realise something happens, just by noticing it, your breathing might actually slow down and you'll find yourself taking slower breaths. And now turn your attention to how the air fills your lungs and your chest, and remember that your lungs go all the way down to your belly, so notice how as you fill your lungs, your whole tummy rises, not just your chest. Notice how your tummy rises as the air goes in . . . and lowers as the air goes out.*

And now I want you to become aware that each time you breathe out, your whole body becomes more relaxed, so with each out-breath your body relaxes and your muscles feel looser and every part of your body becomes floppier. You'll see how your shoulders start to sink down as you become more and more relaxed with each and every out breath, your whole body is becoming more relaxed, more loose and your body is feeling floppier and heavier. All the different parts of your body are becoming heavier as you become more relaxed and more comfortable.

Now I want you to pay attention to different parts of your body. I'm going to start with your toes and work all the way up to your head. It's very easy, you're not going to have to move anything, unless you want to so that you can feel more comfortable. I just want you to pay attention to different parts of your body. So first of all, pay attention to your feet and notice where they are in contact with the floor. Just by paying attention to that, you might start feeling a strange sensation in your feet. Maybe they will start to tingle, or maybe your feet will start to feel heavier and looser and more relaxed. I'd like you to really focus on that feeling now, really focus on the way that your feet are feeling heavier, as if they're full up with some heavy liquid. And really allow that feeling to grow, and get bigger and bigger.

And now let that feeling grow more and start to move up your legs – notice how as you turn your attention to your calves and shins that feeling grows, as if your body is being filled with a liquid, so your calves are beginning to feel heavy, like balloons full of water. Let the feeling get bigger and bigger. Notice how the feeling grows up to your knees and you're feeling your legs becoming more and more relaxed, it goes up your thighs, all the way to your hips. Each time you breathe out, your body is feeling heavier, more relaxed, more floppy and more loose.

Now notice how this feeling goes up from your waist to your tummy, filling your tummy and your chest, everything becoming more relaxed. Now think about your shoulders. I want you just to notice now any particular little knots or stones of tension in your shoulders. And notice how as the feeling of relaxation that's crept up your body, reaches those little knots, each time you breathe out the tension begins to fade away, and the feeling of tightness gets smaller and smaller while the feeling of relaxation gets bigger and bigger. Just focus your attention on that now and then imagine the feeling of relaxation spreading down your arms, through your elbows, down to your hands and eventually right down to your fingertips. Spend a few moments now focusing on your fingertips and how that feeling reaches your fingers, so that everything is becoming looser and heavier and more and more relaxed.

And now turn your attention to your neck. Sometimes in our necks we hold little pockets of tension, or tightness. I want you to just notice any of those and then let that feeling of relaxation that has come over your whole body begin to make those little pockets of tension disappear, fade away. If there's any particularly difficult pockets of tension, you might have to think about your breathing again and each time you breathe out the tension gets smaller and the relaxation gets bigger.

And then allow that feeling, that lovely warm, heavy feeling to creep up the rest of your head, so it's around your jaw, up to your ears, behind your eyes and eventually reaching the top of your head. By now the whole of your body is feeling really heavy, really relaxed, really loose.

Now I want you just to do a little 'body scan', and just notice from your feet all the way up to your head if there's any part of your body that doesn't feel relaxed, any part of your body where there is a little bit of tension left. Focus on that now; focus on the feeling that's throughout the rest of your body, the much bigger, more powerful feeling of relaxation and looseness. Just let that feeling take over any little pockets of tension, just like a sugar lump dissolving in a cup of coffee, or a balloon with the air slowly coming out. Notice how the tension just disappears so that you feel really relaxed now. Feel as if your body is sinking into the floor and chair, all the tension is just disappearing.

In a few moments, I'll be asking you to open your eyes but just for now begin to focus your thoughts on the outside of your body, where it's in contact with the floor or the chair. Then broaden your focus so that you become more aware of the room. Remember some of the things in the room, become aware of the noises here. Just listen now to the sounds of everyday life. In a moment I'll count slowly from three to one. And as I get to one I want you to open your eyes, feeling good, relaxed and completely normal, able to remember everything and happy to talk about your experience. So, remember when I get to one I want you to open your eyes. Three:- beginning to feel lighter, beginning to feel more wide awake and alert, getting ready for the rest of the day and the rest of the week. Two:- feeling even lighter, feeling good, still relaxed but more alert. And one:- feeling wide awake. I'd like you to open your eyes in your own time and gather your thoughts.

Special Place Script

Remember to adapt this so that it suits your child. Ask them to think of a special place that would make them feel relaxed, calm, peaceful, safe and secure. Somewhere their body can take a rest and be loose and floppy and their mind can take a break. It can be real or imaginary or a mixture of both. Spend a bit of time finding out about it. You could write down the details with them, or get them to draw a picture of it. You can use the prompts below to help your child to really fill in the details.

Don't forget to use the tone and speed of your voice to help them to relax.

Where would be a good place to go to feel really safe and comfortable?

It might be a real place or an imagined one. Somewhere that you can feel peaceful, calm and relaxed.

What would that place be like? (allow them to talk freely, if necessary encourage them to elaborate – the following questions might be useful):

What would you see there?

What colours would things be?

What would be to your right / left?

How exactly would you be relaxing there?

Who else would be there?

What would they be doing?

What would you be able to hear?

What would you be able to smell?

What would you be able to touch? How would it feel?

Is the place warm or cold?

What else can you tell me about this place?

Then, if they want to, you can help them to 'visit' their special place in their minds. Use the following as a guide if you want to.

It was so interesting to hear all about your special place. What we're going to do now is do some relaxation. And we're going to think about your special place, which will help you to feel even more relaxed and even safer and even happier.

So, can you get really comfortable? You might need to just shuffle a bit so that you can get really comfy. And it doesn't matter if you need to move a little bit just to make yourself more comfortable while we're doing this, you don't have to sit super still all the time. So, when you're comfortable, if you are happy to do it, close your eyes, you'll find this makes it easier to concentrate on the feelings inside your body, but if you're not happy closing your eyes, that's fine as well. And of course you might change your mind as we go along – which is fine.

Then first of all just notice the noises around us, maybe you can hear people in the street, or maybe there are noises outside the window, or maybe there are some noises in the room that you can hear. Pay attention to those And then gradually bring your attention in, so that you're paying attention to things that are going on inside your own body rather than outside. And the first thing I'd like you to pay attention to is your breathing. I don't want you to do anything to it, just notice the way that you breathe, the way that you breathe in . . . and breathe out.

[Try to match the timing of your words to their actual breathing in and breathing out.]

Feel the air going in through your nose and mouth, down your throat and filling your lungs. And then going out. And as you're noticing your breathing, you'll realise something very strange happens, just through the act of noticing it, your breathing will actually slow down and you'll find yourself taking bigger and bigger breaths. And now turn your attention to how the air fills your lungs and your chest, and remember that your lungs go all the way down to your belly, so notice how if you really fill your lungs, your whole tummy rises, not just your chest. Notice how your tummy rises as the air goes in. And lowers as the air goes out.

And now start feeling your body becoming more and more relaxed. Each time you breathe out your body sinks down and becomes a little more loose, feeling more comfortable, more relaxed, more chilled out, all the tension just disappearing. And notice any little bits of tightness or tension. Focus on those for a few moments and let the feelings of relaxation wash over them and make them disappear, so that each time you breathe out your body becomes heavier and looser, feeling more easy and more relaxed.

And now in your mind, I want you to go to the top of some steps; they can be some real steps that you know, or just some steps that you've made up. Find yourself at the top of these steps, it doesn't matter how many there are, that's up to you. But know that at the bottom of these steps is your special place that you've told me all about. In a moment I'm going to count from five down to one. And as I do that I want you to walk down the steps, so that by the time I get to one, you're at the bottom of the steps, it doesn't matter, it doesn't have to be one step for every count but just find yourself at the bottom of the steps by the time I get to one. So, at the top of the steps, feeling very relaxed, getting ready to go to your special place. Five – feeling more relaxed. Four – feeling heavier and looser. Three – becoming even more relaxed. Two – getting near to your special place. And one – so now find yourself in that special place that we talked about. See those things that you told me about, hear the sounds, smell the smells, feel all the sensations, which go with this scene. I want you to have a good look around, look all around and notice the things that you can see. Become aware of what you're wearing, or whether you're standing or sitting, what colour are your clothes? What can you feel on your skin? Think about the sounds there are, either close to you or further away, and the smells, pay attention now to the smells. Think now about who else is with you, or are you alone? If you are with other people, what are they doing? What are they saying?

[Use the details that your child told you about to enhance the vividness of this imagery.]

And now while you're in this special place, I want you to think about the feelings that go with it, think about how safe and content and relaxed and happy you feel. This is a very special place and going there in your mind can make you feel all these lovely feelings, just enjoy being there for a few moments while I be quiet, and then I'll start talking to you again shortly.

Okay in a few moments I'm going to ask you to come back from your special place, but before you leave it, I wonder if there's something there that you can bring back with you? A little something that will remind you of the place. If there is, just pick it up and put it in your pocket and have one last good look around, this special place will always be there if you want to go back to it, but for now it's time to come back. So in a few moments from now but not quite yet, I'm going to be asking you to come back, so just make your way to the bottom of the steps. If you're bringing something back with you then make sure you've got that and in a few moments I'm going to count from one up to five, and as I do so I'd like you to walk back up the steps so that when I get to five you're at the top of the steps and then I'd like you to open your eyes in your own time and gather your thoughts. So, one, at the bottom of the steps, about to leave your special place. Two, walking away from the special place, feeling a little more wide awake and alert. Three, beginning to think about the room and becoming aware of the noises around you. Four, feeling more wide awake, more alert, knowing that you're here in the room sitting on a . . . [Insert here whatever they are sitting on]. *And five, in your own time, open your eyes and gather your thoughts, feeling wide awake.*

Appendix 3: Sources of Additional Support, Resources and Information

I've listed here some books and organisations that offer information, resources and additional support.

However, if you feel that you or your child are struggling and need more, your GP or family doctor might be a good place to start to find access to additional sources of support such as counselling or therapy if that is what is needed. For yourself, if you live in England you can usually refer yourself directly to the local NHS talking therapies service (search online for NHS Improving Access to Psychological Therapies service or IAPT).

In many countries, schools are getting much more involved in supporting children and families. It's likely that they would also be able to provide some support, or signpost you to other sources of additional support.

Books and booklets

Helping your child

Looking after your child following trauma. A short free guide produced by Greater Manchester Resilience Hub. Available from https://www.penninecare.nhs.uk/trauma

A guide to understanding and managing trauma. A short free guide directly for children and young people produced by Greater Manchester Resilience Hub. Available from https://www.penninecare.nhs.uk/trauma

Helping your child with a physical health condition by Mandy Bryon and Penny Titman. https://overcoming.co.uk/1594/Helping-Your-Child-with-a-Physical-Health-Condition

Helping your child with friendship problems and bullying by Sandra Dunsmuir, Jessica Dewey & Susan Birch. https://overcoming.co.uk/1593/Helping-Your-Child-with-Friendship-Problems-and-Bullying

Support for yourself

An Introduction to Coping with Stress by Lee Brosan. https://overcoming.co.uk/672/An-Introduction-To-Coping-With-Stress---Brosan

How to Cope when your Child Can't by Roz Shafran, Ursula Saunders and Alice Welham. https://overcoming.co.uk/1621/How-To-Cope-When-Your-Child-Cant

There are also other ideas and resources here: https://overcoming.co.uk

Organisations

Child Mental Health

Young Minds
UK charity that supports parents and carers who are concerned about their child's mental health.

Provides helpline, webchat, email and online resources.

www.youngminds.org.uk/parent   0808 802 5544

Papyrus
UK charity dedicated to the prevention of suicide and the promotion of positive mental health and emotional wellbeing in young people.

Provides helpline and resources for children, young people and concerned others. including the guide 'Supporting your child: Self-harm and Suicide'

https://www.papyrus-uk.org/   0800 068 4141

Trauma

NSPCC (National Society for the Prevention of Cruelty to Children)
Expert advice and support, particularly if you are worried about a child being abused. Including resources about children's mental health and self-harm.

Provides helpline, resources and email.

www.nspcc.org.uk   0808 800 5000

UK Trauma Council (UKTC)

A charitable project that brings together leading experts in child trauma (academics, clinicians, policy advisors and those with lived experience) from across the UK to produce free resources and guidance to support anyone working to nurture and protect children and young people following trauma.

Provides articles, animations, videos, guidance, handouts, presentations, and training.

www.uktraumacouncil.org

Beacon House

A UK specialist therapeutic service.

Provides free resources providing knowledge about the repair of trauma and adversity for those who need it.

https://beaconhouse.org.uk/resources/

National Child Traumatic Stress Network (NCTSN)

A US based network of child trauma services and resources.

Provides a huge range of free resources about child trauma for various different audiences.

https://www.nctsn.org/

Bereavement and Loss

The following organisations all have UK-wide coverage. As well as providing direct support, they all have up-to-date reading lists of additional books that might be useful. You may well have a local child bereavement service that would be worth contacting too. The Child Bereavement Network   (https://childhoodbereavementnetwork.org.uk/) provides a searchable directory that will help you to find a local child bereavement service.

Child Bereavement UK (CBUK)

A UK charity offering support, information and guidance to parents and carers after a bereavement.

Provides helpline, webchat and email.

www.childbereavementuk.org   0800 028 8840

Winston's Wish

A UK charity offering advice and guidance for parents and carers of grieving children.

Provides a helpline and email.

www.winstonswish.org   0808 802 0021

Grief Encounter

A UK charity offering help, guidance and advice for parent and carers of bereaved children.

Provides helpline, webchat and email.

www.griefencounter.org.uk   0808 802 0111

Other services

There is a directory of services available here https://
www.annafreud.org/on-my-mind/youth-wellbeing/ that
might help to identify some local services.

Appendix 4: References – Research and Articles

Below is a list of research that I have referred to throughout the book.

1   Fauth, B., Thompson, M., & Penny, A. (2009). Associations between childhood bereavement and children's background, experiences and outcomes. *London: National Children's Bureau.*

2   Burns, M., Griese, B., King, S., & Talmi, A. (2020). Childhood bereavement: Understanding prevalence and related adversity in the United States. *American Journal of Orthopsychiatry, 90*(4), 391.

3   Lewis, S. J., Arseneault, L., Caspi, A., Fisher, H. L., Matthews, T., Moffitt, T. E., . . . & Danese, A. (2019). The epidemiology of trauma and post-traumatic stress disorder in a representative cohort of young people in England and Wales. *The Lancet Psychiatry, 6*(3), 247–56.

4   American Psychiatric Association. (2022) *Diagnostic and statistical manual of mental disorders, fifth edition,*

text revision. Washington: American Psychiatric Association.

5   Copeland, W. E., Keeler, G., Angold, A., & Costello, E. J. (2007). Traumatic events and post-traumatic stress in childhood. *Archives of general psychiatry, 64*(5), 577–84.

6   Wethington, H. R., Hahn, R. A., Fuqua-Whitley, D. S., Sipe, T. A., Crosby, A. E., Johnson, R. L., . . . & Task Force on Community Preventive Services. (2008). The effectiveness of interventions to reduce psychological harm from traumatic events among children and adolescents: a systematic review. *American journal of preventive medicine, 35*(3), 287–313.

7   Bonanno, G. A. (2005). Resilience in the face of potential trauma. *Current directions in psychological science, 14*(3), 135–8.

8   Alisic, E., Zalta, A. K., Van Wesel, F., Larsen, S. E., Hafstad, G. S., Hassanpour, K., & Smid, G. E. (2014). Rates of post-traumatic stress disorder in trauma-exposed children and adolescents: meta-analysis. *The British Journal of Psychiatry, 204*(5), 335–40.

9   Hiller, R. M., Meiser-Stedman, R., Fearon, P., Lobo, S., McKinnon, A., Fraser, A., & Halligan, S. L. (2016). Research Review: Changes in the prevalence and symptom severity of child post-traumatic stress disorder in the year following trauma–A meta-analytic study. *Journal of Child Psychology and Psychiatry, 57*(8), 884–98.

10   McKay, M. T., Cannon, M., Chambers, D., Conroy, R. M., Coughlan, H., Dodd, P., Healy, C., O'Donnell, L., & Clarke, M. C. (2021). Childhood trauma and adult mental disorder: A systematic review and meta-analysis of longitudinal cohort studies. *Acta psychiatrica Scandinavica, 143*(3), 189–205.

11   Alisic, E., Zalta, A. K., Van Wesel, F., Larsen, S. E., Hafstad, G. S., Hassanpour, K., & Smid, G. E. (2014). Rates of post-traumatic stress disorder in trauma-exposed children and adolescents: meta-analysis. *The British Journal of Psychiatry, 204*(5), 335–40.

12   Goleman, D. (1996). *Emotional intelligence: Why it can matter more than IQ.* Bloomsbury Publishing.

13   Vibhakar, V., Allen, L. R., Gee, B., & Meiser-Stedman, R. (2019). A systematic review and meta-analysis on the prevalence of depression in children and adolescents after exposure to trauma. *Journal of affective disorders, 255,* 77–89.

14   Smith, P., Yule, W., Perrin, S., Tranah, T., Dalgleish, T. I. M., & Clark, D. M. (2007). Cognitive-behavioral therapy for PTSD in children and adolescents: A preliminary randomized controlled trial. *Journal of the American Academy of Child & Adolescent Psychiatry, 46*(8), 1051–61.

15   Berkowitz, S. J., Stover, C. S., & Marans, S. R. (2011). The child and family traumatic stress intervention: Secondary prevention for youth at risk of developing PTSD. *Journal of Child Psychology and Psychiatry, 52*(6), 676–85.

16   American Psychiatric Association. (2022) *Diagnostic and statistical manual of mental disorders, fifth edition, text revision*. Washington: American Psychiatric Association.

and

World Health Organization. (2019). *ICD-11: International classification of diseases (11th revision)*. https://icd.who.int/browse11

17   Meiser-Stedman, R. (2002). Towards a cognitive–behavioral model of PTSD in children and adolescents. *Clinical child and family psychology review*, *5*(4), 217–32.

18   Georgina Gómez de La Cuesta , Susanne Schweizer , Julia Diehle , Judith Young & Richard Meiser-Stedman (2019) The relationship between maladaptive appraisals and posttraumatic stress disorder: a meta-analysis, European Journal of Psychotraumatology, 10:1, 1620084, DOI: 10.1080/20008198.2019.1620084

19   Mavranezouli, I., Megnin-Viggars, O., Daly, C., Dias, S., Stockton, S., Meiser-Stedman, R., ... & Pilling, S. (2020). Research Review: Psychological and psychosocial treatments for children and young people with post-traumatic stress disorder: a network meta-analysis. *Journal of child psychology and psychiatry*, *61*(1), 18–29.

20   Brewin, C. R., Gregory, J. D., Lipton, M., & Burgess, N. (2010). Intrusive images in psychological disorders: characteristics, neural mechanisms, and treatment implications. *Psychological review*, *117*(1), 210.

21   Richards, D., & Lovell, K. (1999). Behavioural and cognitive behavioural interventions in the treatment of PTSD. In W. Yule (Ed.), *Post-traumatic stress disorders: Concepts and therapy* (pp. 239–66). John Wiley & Sons Ltd.

22   Ehlers, A. & Clark, D. M., (2000). A Cognitive Model of PTSD. Behaviour, *Research and Therapy, 38,* 319–45.

23   Alisic, E., Zalta, A. K., Van Wesel, F., Larsen, S. E., Hafstad, G. S., Hassanpour, K., & Smid, G. E. (2014). Rates of post-traumatic stress disorder in trauma-exposed children and adolescents: meta-analysis. *The British Journal of Psychiatry, 204*(5), 335–40.

24   Fauth, B., Thompson, M., & Penny, A. (2009). Associations between childhood bereavement and children's background, experiences and outcomes. *London: National Children's Bureau.*

25   Dowdney, L. (2000). Annotation: Childhood bereavement following parental death. *The Journal of Child Psychology and Psychiatry and Allied Disciplines, 41*(7), 819–30.

26   Worden, J. W. (2018). Grief counseling and grief therapy. A handbook for the mental health practitioner (5th ed.). Springer Publishing.

27   Schut, M. Schut. H. (1999). The dual process model of coping with bereavement: Rationale and description. *Death studies, 23*(3), 197–224.

28 Hobfoll, S. E., Watson, P., Bell, C. C., Bryant, R. A., Brymer, M. J., Friedman, M. J., . . . & Ursano, R. J. (2007). Five essential elements of immediate and mid–term mass trauma intervention: Empirical evidence. *Psychiatry*, *70*(4), 283–315.

29 Hiller, R. M., Meiser-Stedman, R., Lobo, S., Creswell, C., Fearon, P., Ehlers, A., . . . & Halligan, S. L. (2018). A longitudinal investigation of the role of parental responses in predicting children's post-traumatic distress. *Journal of Child Psychology and Psychiatry*, *59*(7), 781–9.

30 Lieberman, M. D., Eisenberger, N. I., Crockett, M. J., Tom, S. M., Pfeifer, J. H., & Way, B. M. (2007). Putting feelings into words. *Psychological science*, *18*(5), 421–8.

31 Trickey, D., Siddaway, A. P., Meiser-Stedman, R., Serpell, L., & Field, A. P. (2012). A meta-analysis of risk factors for post-traumatic stress disorder in children and adolescents. *Clinical psychology review*, *32*(2), 122–38.

32 Schnall, S., Harber, K. D., Stefanucci, J. K., & Proffitt, D. R. (2008). Social support and the perception of geographical slant. *Journal of experimental social psychology*, *44*(5), 1246–55.

33 Coan, J. A., Schaefer, H. S., & Davidson, R. J. (2006). Lending a hand: Social regulation of the neural response to threat. *Psychological science*, *17*(12), 1032–9.

34 Andretta, J. R., & McKay, M. T. (2020). Self-efficacy and well-being in adolescents: A comparative study using

variable and person-centered analyses. *Children and Youth Services Review, 118,* 105374.

and Caprara, G. V., Steca, P., Gerbino, M., Paciello, M., & Vecchio, G. M. (2006). Looking for adolescents' well-being: Self-efficacy beliefs as determinants of positive thinking and happiness. *Epidemiology and Psychiatric Sciences, 15*(1), 30–43.

35   Antonovsky, A. (1987). *Unraveling the mystery of health: How people manage stress and stay well.* Jossey-bass.

36   Pfefferbaum, B., Nixon, S. J., Tivis, R. D., Doughty, D. E., Pynoos, R. S., Gurwitch, R. H., & Foy, D. W. (2001). Television exposure in children after a terrorist incident. *Psychiatry, 64*(3), 202–11.

37   Joseph, S. (2012). What doesn't kill us. *Psychologist 25,* 816–9.

38   UNESCO New SDG 4 Data on Bullying http://uis.unesco.org/en/news/new-sdg-4-data-bullying

39   Radford, L., Corral, S., Bradley, C., Fisher, H., Bassett, C., Howat, N., & Collishaw, S. (2011). *Child abuse and neglect in the UK today.* NSPCC.

40   Merrick, M. T., Ford, D. C., Ports, K. A., & Guinn, A. S. (2018). Prevalence of adverse childhood experiences from the 2011–2014 behavioral risk factor surveillance system in 23 states. *JAMA pediatrics, 172*(11), 1038–44.

41   McCrory, E. J., De Brito, S. A., Sebastian, C. L., Mechelli, A., Bird, G., Kelly, P. A., & Viding, E. (2011).

Heightened neural reactivity to threat in child victims of family violence. *Current Biology*, *21*(23), R947-R948.

42   Office for National Statistics (2019). *Crime Survey for England and Wales (CSEW)*.

43   Finkelhor, D., Shattuck, A., Turner, H. A., & Hamby, S. L. (2014). The lifetime prevalence of child sexual abuse and sexual assault assessed in late adolescence. *Journal of Adolescent Health*, *55*(3), 329–33.

44   Mental Health of Children and Young People in England, 2017 [PAS] https://digital.nhs.uk/data-and-information/publications/statistical/mental-health-of-children-and-young-people-in-england/2017/2017

45   Trickey, D., Siddaway, A. P., Meiser-Stedman, R., Serpell, L., & Field, A. P. (2012). A meta-analysis of risk factors for post-traumatic stress disorder in children and adolescents. *Clinical psychology review*, *32*(2), 122–38.

Acknowledgements

I would like to thank all the children, young people and families who I have worked with. They have taught me so much about what helps them to recover, and I feel incredibly fortunate to have had the opportunity to learn from them.

I would also like to thank those academics and practitioners who have done so much to increase our understanding of trauma and bereavement, so that we have much better evidence-based ideas about what helps. In particular, I would like to thank Bill Yule, Richard Meiser-Stedman, Patrick Smith, Sean Perrin, Rachel Hiller, Eamon McCrory, Nick Grey, Kerry Young, Beck Ferrari and Dora Black. Thank you to Polly Waite and Andrew McAleer for their encouragement, their help putting this book together, and their seemingly unending patience. Thank you to my co-author Vicky Lawson, without whom I would still be writing drafts. Finally, I would like to thank my friends and family who have been so supportive throughout the process, particularly my dad (I think Mum would have been beside herself with pride), my partner and my two amazing children.

Index

Page numbers in *italic* refer to diagrams